THE TRANSFORMATION SERIES

‖‖ ‖‖‖ ‖‖‖‖‖‖‖ ‖ ‖‖‖ ‖‖‖‖‖‖‖‖‖‖‖‖ ‖‖

Gay Hendricks, *General Editor*

✓ **S0-AVU-149**

Books in the Transformation Series explore the transitions of
human life and the possibilities for happier, more creative living
through the application of the psychology of adjustment

BOOKS IN THE SERIES:

PRENTICE-HALL INTERNATIONAL, INC., *London*
PRENTICE-HALL OF AUSTRALIA PTY. LIMITED, *Sydney*
PRENTICE-HALL OF CANADA, LTD., *Toronto*
PRENTICE-HALL OF INDIA PRIVATE LIMITED, *New Delhi*
PRENTICE-HALL OF JAPAN, INC., *Tokyo*
PRENTICE-HALL OF SOUTHEAST ASIA PTE. LTD., *Singapore*
WHITEHALL BOOKS LIMITED, *Wellington, New Zealand*

A CONDITIONING PROGRAM FOR YOUR MIND

The centered athlete

Gay Hendricks and Jon Carlson

A SPECTRUM BOOK

PRENTICE-HALL, INC., Englewood Cliffs, New Jersey 07632

Library of Congress Cataloging in Publication Data

HENDRICKS. GAY.
   The centered athlete.

   (The Transformation series)
   "A Spectrum Book."
   Includes bibliographical references and index.
   1. Sports—Psychological aspects. I. Carlson. Jon.
II. Title.
GV706.4.H46   796'.01   81-15317
                           AACR2

ISBN 0-13-122218-X

ISBN 0-13-122200-7 {PBK.}

For My Teachers Laura, Kirstin, Matthew, Karin
and the Centered Athletes of the 1979-1981
University of Wisconsin-Whitewater Cross Country teams.
—*Jon*

For Coach Jack Love.
—*Gay*

10 9 8 7 6 5 4 3 2 1

Editorial/production supervision and interior design by Carol Smith
Manufacturing buyer: Cathie Lenard

This Spectrum Book is available to businesses and organizations
at a special discount when ordered in large quantities.
For information, contact Prentice-Hall, Inc., General Book Marketing,
Special Sales Division, Englewood Cliffs, N.J. 07632.

Contents

vi

Preface

Athletics are for fun, fitness, and feeling better about ourselves; they can help us relax, enjoy companionship, and find civilized outlets for aggressive impulses. Athletics are also a path we can take to learn about the larger game of life. Through athletics, it is possible to expand our ability to handle the game of life in ways that bring satisfaction and creativity to ourselves and the people with whom we live and work. A feeling of personal power results when the athlete learns how to remain calm, centered, comfortable, and confident in traditionally stressful situations. The centered athlete has discovered new options and attitudes—feeling clear-headed, naturally high, light and powerful—and has learned to experience the sounds, smells, sights, and colors as he or she participates. Through altered perceptions, a new sensitivity to life is created.

This book provides ideas and exercises that will allow the athlete to move into a new dimension through the use of the psychological techniques of centering, imagery breath control, and expansion. It is only within this decade that professional, Olympic, and other world-class athletes have begun to realize the benefits of these methods. Improved performance, increased enjoyment, and heightened awareness are the likely end-products.

We would like to thank and recognize a lifetime friend, John Johnson, for his editorial assistance and Nancy Williamson for her sensitive renderings that inspired the art.

Gay Hendricks, Ph.D.   *John Carlson, Ph.D.*
Colorado Springs, Colorado   *Lake Geneva, Wisconsin*

1

Centering, sports, and the game of life

Sports are for fun, fitness, and feeling better about ourselves; they help us relax, enjoy companionship, and find civilized outlets for the aggressive impulses of that ancient gorilla that resides within.

Sports are also a path we can take to learning about the larger game of life. Through sports it is possible to expand our ability to handle the game of life in ways that bring satisfaction and creativity to ourselves and the people around us. Sports are a way of getting free of the limitations of the past, coming into the here and now, and using the limitless space of the present for our ultimate fulfillment. In short, sports are for centering.

The term *centering* seems to have come originally from the craft of pottery. In that craft there is an intimate and immediate relationship between the potter's inner feeling of centeredness and the pot that he is creating. If the potter is feeling off-center within, it is difficult to create a balanced and symmetrical pot. When he comes into harmony with himself, the inner feeling of centeredness immediately manifests in a harmonious creation. So it is with sports, and with life.

In sports it is equally easy to see the relationship between our inner self and the self we are expressing in the game that is being played. In each swing of the tennis racquet, for example, in the way the body is held and the way the racquet meets the ball, it is possible for the player to learn about his relationship with life itself. In each mile the runner covers, in the way she breathes, the swing of the stride, and the fall of the foot, there are all of the lessons she needs to learn about not only the way she runs but the way she runs her life.

Successful athletes do not play to escape life. How could they? The game is life, and life is a game. We are all ultimately in quest of the same thing: To find our true selves and to express our deepest love and creativity in ways that enrich ourselves and the world. We carry the self with us when we play sports. We can choose to deny and ignore learning about ourselves while we play, or we can choose to make sports an arena for finding out who we are, dissolving our limitations, and expressing ourselves most creatively. If we choose the latter the possibilities are limitless.

The psychologist Abraham Maslow made an important observation some years ago when he described what has come to be called Maslow's Hierarchy of Needs (illustrated below). In essence he said that human needs are arranged as on a pyramid, the more basic needs supporting higher needs. He also described two sorts of needs that psychology had not dealt with before and that have tremendous implications for sports.

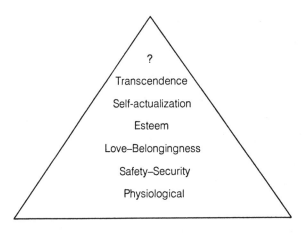

Physiological needs are at the base of the pyramid. If physical needs are not met it is difficult to focus on any higher need. If we are hungry or cold, in other words, our highest priority is to remedy those conditions.

The next level comprises the needs for safety and security. If we are meeting physical needs then our next priority is to feel safe. Until we feel safe and secure it is unlikely that we will turn our attention to meeting the needs in the middle of the pyramid: love, belongingness, esteem.

Love, belonging, and esteem have been called the ego needs because they help give us an identity. The term *ego* simply means *I*, so the ego needs can be seen as those that give us a sense of ourselves as unique and valuable beings.

Until Maslow most psychologists stopped there. Human beings, they thought, could be defined in terms of physical needs or by the quest to meet ego needs. Not so, said Maslow, for when ego needs are met the human being strives to meet even higher needs. The focus is on what Maslow called self-actualization.

Self-actualization is our attempt to find the true self, who we really are; to express that self; and to enjoy relationship and all of life from the space of that self. It is a commitment to finding how we are limiting ourselves, then dissolving those limitations and going for the highest we can be.

Maslow also described the ultimate need as one for transcendence. The final reach of the self is for oneness, unity with all. It is the need to go beyond the ego and the self, to melt into something larger than oneself.

Listen to a description of transcendence by one of the greatest runners of all time, Roger Bannister:

> *I remember a moment when I stood barefoot on firm dry sand by the sea. The air had a special quality as if it had a life of its own. The sound of breakers on the shore shut out all others. I looked up at the clouds, like great white-sailed galleons, chasing proudly inland. I looked down at the regular ripples on the sand, and could not absorb so much beauty. I was taken aback—each of the myriad particles of sand was perfect in its way. I looked more closely, hoping perhaps that my eyes might detect some flaw. But for once there was nothing to detract from all this beauty.*
>
> *In this supreme moment I leapt in sheer joy. I was startled, and frightened, by the tremendous excitement that so few steps could create. I glanced round uneasily to see if anyone was watching. A few more steps—self-consciously now and firmly gripping the original excitement. The earth seemed almost to move with me. I was running now, and a fresh rhythm entered my body. No longer conscious of my move-*

ment I discovered a new unity with nature. I had found a new source of power and beauty, a source I never dreamt existed.*

Here is an example of transcendence in tennis, contributed by an amateur player of the authors' acquaintance:

> *Here comes the serve. I am lost in it. It is a moment of keeping my eye completely on the ball. Nothing else exists: we are one. We meet, ball and racquet, in a perfect synchrony of form and force. No effort. I hit an uncanny shot that somehow slithers past my opponent's outstretched arm and nicks the court just inches in bounds.*

> *I get set for the next serve. Something feels wrong. Ah, I see that I am still congratulating myself for the last shot. I settle and center just in time to flinch as his serve blasts past, too long. I am spared.*

> *In comes his second serve, a wicked spin that has me flailing for a piece of it. I am there, but not quite there, and my shot strikes the net and dies.*

None of us will ever be centered all of the time. We are not destined to be permanently in the state of self-actualization and transcendence. Centering, then, is not a place to be—it is a way of getting places. We will always be in the process of having it and losing it, then getting it back again.

Athletics is an ideal arena in which to seek self-actualization and transcendence. In sports we can choose a terrain, a court or field that suits us, then play on it in a way that allows us to discover our true potential and ultimately to become one with all of life.

We put a question mark at the top of the pyramid because we can never place a limit on the human potential. When humanity meets the needs for self-actualization and transcendence, higher needs will undoubtedly arise that we can strive to meet.

*Reprinted by permission of Dodd, Mead & Company, Inc. and the author from *The Four-Minute Mile* by Roger Bannister. Copyright © 1955, 1981 by Roger Bannister.

ATTITUDES THAT INVITE SELF-ACTUALIZATION AND TRANSCENDENCE IN SPORTS

What are the key attitudes we can bring to our play, the ways of looking at sports that will allow us to turn athletics into a process of centering, self-actualization, and transcendence? Here are several drawn from discussions with amateur and professional athletes from many different sports.

PLAYING TO BECOME FREE FROM THE LIMITATIONS OF THE PAST   We are all the products of our conditioning. No matter the family or society in which we grew up, we were trained to see things a certain way, to accept certain beliefs as true, to view ourselves and the world around us from the viewpoint of that family or culture. The conditioning from the past has a profound influence on the way we live our lives. One of the things that gives life excitement is spotting and overcoming the limitations of the past. Sports can be an excellent tool in this process. An example can illustrate:

A young man grew up in a family of writers and intellectuals in which very little emphasis was put on keeping one's body fit. He became very fat, so much so that from the 7th to the 10th grade he was allowed to sit out physical education class. He read a book on the sidelines while the others played sports. Sometimes the coach gave him the task of sweeping out the gym and locker room. Things were soon to change, though. A new physical education teacher joined the school in the young man's sophomore year, and surprised the student by refusing to let him sit out. The young man used every argument he could think of to persuade the teacher to let him skip the class. The teacher, however, remained unmoved. So, the student grudgingly began to participate. After an agonizing month of sore muscles and wheezing breath, he began to feel new energy in his body. In fact, he began to look forward to physical education class. By December he was addicted. He was first on the field and last to leave. The joy he felt in discovering his body was evident as his grades improved and his friendships expanded. Most of all, the change was evident

*in the healthy glow on his face and in his rapidly diminishing
waistline. By the end of the year he had lost over fifty pounds.*

*By his senior year he was competing in football and track,
and while he was not a star performer, he won a school medal
for being the person who contributed the most to team spirit.*

Even if we do not begin with a handicap as this young man did we
all have past limitations to be overcome.

On the field of play we have the opportunity to examine all
our beliefs about ourselves and the world and to let go of those
that do not serve us any longer. A tennis player, for example,
might notice that she consistently tends to chalk up large leads,
but then falters and loses the game. If she takes an attitude of
discovering where this tendency comes from, she might recall
that in her family people always started things with a bang but
then let them slide into eventual failure. Since we tend uncon-
sciously to imitate the patterns of behavior we see around us
while growing up, she might see that in her tennis game she is
recreating an old pattern from the past. Further, she might notice
that she plays out the same pattern in other areas of her life.

Playing the game of life well involves the ability to see when
the past is encroaching upon the present. Once spotted, these old
limiting patterns can begin to dissolve. All it takes on our part is a
willingness to be aware of how our past conditioning is getting in
the way of the present.

PLAYING TO BE FREE OF THE PERSONALITY. A second attitude that can
help turn athletics into a process of centering is to see how our
personalities limit us and to use sports as a way of obtaining
freedom from the personality.

The Latin word *persona* is the root of *personality*. It means
mask. One way to look at the personality is to see it as a set of
masks we have learned to use in our lives to meet our needs. The
personality is the collection of masks that we put on to get people
to recognize us and love us. Early in life it is common for us to see
that being ourselves does not get our needs met: People only respond to us when we put on the masks they like. So we oblige, but
in so doing we cover up our true selves. Later in life the person-

ality that worked when we were growing up has to be discarded if we are to find what is true and real about ourselves.

Anyone who has ever played a game or run a mile knows that personality can be one's most formidable opponent. When we begin to exert ourselves the personality begins to emerge. Of course positive aspects of our personalities also emerge: valor, persistence, honor, sportsmanship. But we must consider the negative first.

In sports, as in the rest of life, we encounter personality problems such as

- being overly critical of ourselves
- choking under pressure
- temper tantrums
- discourtesy to opponents
- not having fun.

Sports are an ideal place to spot these troublesome aspects of ourselves. If we can see through them on the field of play we can weed them out before they cause us woe on the larger field of life.

PLAYING TO LEARN THE BIG LESSONS: UNHEALTHY COMPETITION   One of the most troublesome aspects of the personality is the way it handles competition. To understand our unhealthy views of competition and to get free of them can be a major breakthrough in how much we get out of sports as well as how well we become. Someone asked a young tennis player, early in his career, whether his goal was to become really good. After thinking it over for a moment, he said, "No, my goal is to be the most fun to play with." He eventually became a championship player. By focusing his energy away from winning and putting it on the moment-by-moment enjoyment of the game how could he help but become good?

The unhealthy view of competition sees the world from a position of scarcity. There is a scarcity of points, for example, and your job is to get more than your opponent. We can see the same view in our personal lives, where many people see a scarcity of love and recognition, for which they must compete. In this unhealthy view of competition satisfaction is available only if you win, and winning involves defeating someone else.

However, there are two types of satisfaction in the world: results satisfaction and process satisfaction. In results satisfaction we feel good when we have achieved a certain result. The problem with this type of satisfaction is that it has dissatisfaction built into it. One reason is that most of the time we are on our way to achieving a result, not actually achieving it, so that if we tie our good feelings to achieving the result we are doomed to feeling dissatisfied most of the time. Another problem with results satisfaction is that the result is never quite simple enough. We could have done it better or there is the next game to worry about or we did not get a big enough headline. So while we have some satisfaction after the achievement of a result, there is also a sense of dissatisfaction.

Yet another problem with results satisfaction is that in any endeavor we commonly have several results in mind, some that may be totally unconscious. A person may run a marathon for many conscious reasons: to prove to himself he can do it, to get in really good shape, to experience the camaraderie of the race. There may also be unconscious reasons to which he would not readily admit: to impress his girlfriend, to show his father he's a real man, to justify the cost of his running shoes. When the result is achieved, then, there is not total satisfaction because all of the motives have not been acknowledged. We cannot allow ourselves to feel good about achieving something we have not acknowledged we are trying to achieve.

The worst problem of results satisfaction comes when you lose. In loss the sense of dissatisfaction is so great that it must usually be shared. So we blame it on the weather, the ball, the underhanded play of our opponent, a broken shoelace, the enmity of a referee. And even that doesn't help. The search for reasons and excuses, especially in front of the TV cameras, sometimes reaches ludicrous proportions. How refreshed we are when we hear a losing coach say, "They played better than we did."

Process satisfaction is of an entirely different character. It is the art of being satisfied with the process of playing the game. With process satisfaction we are in total control of satisfaction with the moment-by-moment unfoldment of the game, unlike results satisfaction over which many things (like the opponents and the weather) may exert control.

It is possible then to feel satisfied with everything that happens during sports or the game of life. We can feel satisfied with playing squalidly, if our attitude is that we are learning from it. Once we commit ourselves to enjoying and learning from each moment we take the energy off the result and put it on the moment, where it belongs. By doing so we will most likely achieve better results as well.

A NEW VIEW OF COMPETITION   Here is a new way of looking at competition. It is based on process satisfaction rather than on scarcity consciousness. Instead of focusing on winning or defeating the opponent (or the clock, as in running) focus instead on the moment-by-moment enjoyment of the game. When you find yourself outside the here and now bring yourself back to the present and push the satisfaction button. See if you can feel satisfied even with negative experiences like pain or dissatisfaction. Play with the intention of being satisfied with each moment.

Then put your attention on being the most challenging you can be to your opponent or to yourself. Let's use tennis for an example. If you stretch your opponent to the limit, she will have the most fun and learn the most. You will likely beat her, but even if you lose you will feel good about it. The healthy way of competing, then, is to offer your opponent the most challenging lessons about life that you can muster. At the same time you can view your opponent's efforts as opportunities for you to learn to respond with the very highest in you.

LEARNING TO FEEL   A key lesson of life, especially for men, is learning how to experience feelings. In Western culture many people are taught that they should not feel, that there is something wrong, for example, with being scared, sad, or joyful. In other words we are taught to put the brakes on our feelings. The trouble is that putting brakes on does not make the feelings go away. And to hold back on negative feelings means that we must hold back on the positive as well, so that resistance toward feelings cuts down on our ability to enjoy life.

Many people also fall into the mental trap of trying to handle feelings with their minds by using logic.

- I'll feel better tomorrow.
- Keep a stiff upper lip.
- There's nothing to be afraid of.
- Easy, boy.
- Big boys don't cry.

The problem is that feelings are our spontaneous reactions to things. Feelings can be denied or ignored by the mind, but they cannot be eliminated by it. Rather, feelings must be dealt with directly, by experiencing them and trying to understand why they are happening.

Sports are an ideal place to learn how to feel. In the heat of play many feelings come up: anger, fear, exhilaration. The field of play can be a place where feelings can be deeply experienced. If you flush some anger from an old hiding place inside during a run, for example, you can feel it deeply and sprint for a minute to burn up the energy from it. Or, if a wave of fear overtakes you in a tennis game that feeling can be acknowledged, surrendered to, speculated upon, and resolved in the space of a few moments. The key factor in learning to feel is our intention: If we set our minds to learning about ourselves and our feelings we can learn at play as much as or more than we can in the therapist's office.

If we view sports as a place to learn the big lessons of life, such as how to handle competition and how to deal with feelings, we can transform our moment-to-moment play into richly charged moments of learning the lessons we most need to learn. Some of our big lessons are

- how to give and receive love
- how to communicate clearly
- how to make and keep meaningful agreements

- how to control negative thinking
- how to deal with stress
- how to deal with the negativity of others.

Learning these lessons is what life is about, and when we are able to take a broader view of sports we can see that the field of play is an ideal place to learn these and other key lessons.

THE CENTERED ATHLETE

On our way to a permanent state of centeredness the game of life may be played as successive moments of centering. On the field of play the athlete who is committed to centering is in the process of

- getting free of the past
- shedding limiting beliefs
- experiencing feelings
- learning to give and receive
- communicating clearly
- enjoying the moment
- finding the true self
- expanding to experience transcendence.

Perhaps in time, with much practice and a strong commitment to these concepts, we can develop a permanent sense of centered-ness, an ongoing, ever-flowing inner spring of harmony and bal-ance that is not disturbed by loss, or victory, or any of the other vicissitudes of sport or life.

2

In the mind's eye: imagery experiences for centered athletes

Those who do not observe the movements of their own minds must of necessity be unhappy. [Marcus Aurelius]

Argue for your limitations and sure enough, they're yours. [Richard Bach]

Man's imagination is as infinite as the universe: it knows no bounds, has no known limitations. The awareness of discovered imagination is awesome; even more awesome are those discoveries which have yet to be revealed beyond existing frontiers. [Joseph Shorr]

The pictures in (man's) mind are part of his mind as an organ is part of his body, are indispensable to the life of the mind as the heart is to the body. [Sylvia Ashton Warner]

Whatever they had believed about themselves, they had become. Our beliefs about ourselves and our world govern all our experience. Our images are self-fulfilling prophecies. What we envision is what we get. [Adelaide Bry]

Become the vision that you have of your body. [Arnold Schwarzenegger]

HOW THE MIND AFFECTS THE BODY

Visualization procedures are hardly new. The summoning and holding of certain images in the mind for examination and exploration can be traced to ancient Egypt, to shaman rituals from many cultures, the various schools of yoga and meditation, the Oriental martial arts, and to classical hypnosis. The notion of mental imagery, visualization, seeing with the mind's eye, or inner vision (or whatever one chooses to call the introspective process accompanied by visual images) has an extraordinarily rich history in both psychology and medicine. Forming the basis for study in the first psychological laboratory established by Wundt in 1879, the scientific analysis of content of the mind seemed to be an appropriate area of research for the fledgling discipline as psychologists attempted to objectify the nebulous arena of the imagination. Early results being neither pragmatic nor interpretable, psychologists turned to the analysis of behavior as their focus, dismissing the more phenomenological aspects once again as grist for the theologians and philosophers.

Jacobsen's (1942) work had a pronounced effect on our understanding of the physiological ramifications of mental imagery. His research has indicated that during imagery there is measurable tension in the part of the body involved in the visualization. Tension appears for example, in the muscles of the eye during visual imagery, the muscles of speech during subvocal thought, and in the leg muscles when one imagines running.

The physiological effects of the mental imagery process have also been documented by Schultz and Luthe (1969) in their compilation of 2,400 studies on the use of autogenic therapy. This therapeutic technique involves visualization and relaxation procedures within a highly structured framework. Changes accompanying the procedures include alterations in body temperature, blood sugar, blood pressure, white blood cell count, and brain wave patterns. However, as many of these changes occur naturally by relaxation alone, the relationship between visualization and relaxation and the relative contribution of each to the end result is still unclear.

In recent years biofeedback research has demonstrated that individuals can learn to control various physiological functions through appropriate visualization. Relief from pain, warming or cooling of parts of the body, control of blood flow, and muscular relaxation can all be mastered through biofeedback training. Simply hoping to raise the temperature of your hands will probably have no effect. But if you visualize yourself standing in front of a fireplace warming your hands, or imagine yourself in a hot tub, their temperature may change quickly.

Internal processes influence performance; their purposeful direction and control can expand one's skills and enjoyment. Many athletes become aware of the inner conflicts that affect their performance. In the long run it is not enough for athletes to be aware of their inner conflicts: They must change the way visualization and definition occurs. The resolution of an internal conflict is more important than a mere solution; steroids remove pain; sedatives offer a solution to anxiety; refusing to schedule difficult opponents offers a solution to an unpleasant encounter. But in none of these cases has the actual problem been solved.

Superficial solutions are easily conceived, prescribed, and used in athletics. These allow one to perform on a short-term basis, but they usually have the side effects of further injury to the existing problem and/or the development of new symptoms.

Imagery is defined as "mental pictures that have organized themselves into some kind of pattern." During the image-making process, people react to the world they see and, like artists in the act of painting a picture, give organization and meaning to these images (Khatena, 1975). For every movement, every muscle, every injury, we have a mental picture of what is to be done or is occurring. For permanent change to take place images must be modified or expanded: For the runner whose finishing kick is always weak, the golfer who can never shoot well on a certain hole, the weight lifter who believes 400 pounds is the maximum, a review of their reality is in order. An image change can bring about an actual change in performance.

MIND TRAINING IN ATHLETICS

A primary focus of the centering approach to athletics is the mastery of procedures for individual awareness. Combining centering, visualization, and guided imagery deepens one's inner contact while sitting or moving. These processes, when combined with a physical training routine, open pathways for the simultaneous experience of physical, mental, emotional, and spiritual dimensions within. This unified approach to athletic experience will develop greater athletic potential and enjoyment (Spino, 1977, p. 100).

Football players such as O. J. Simpson report that they made important gains in their own play style through the use of mental concentration. Fran Tarkenton maintains that the physical act of passing the ball is the easiest part in the game.

Golfer Jack Nicklaus gives this a handy label. He calls it "going to the movies." He says that he imagines each shot from start to finish before he actually makes it—mentally setting up, swinging, hitting the ball, seeing it take off, land, roll to a stop. Ben Hogan felt that golf was 20 percent physical and 80 percent mental.

In a recent radio interview, Chris Evert Lloyd was asked how she practiced for a championship tennis match. She stated that in addition to actual practice she carefully and painstakingly re hearses every significant detail of a match in her mind's eye. She thinks about the opponent's style and form, and any maneuvers that person may make during the match. Tim Gallwey's *Inner Tennis* develops an entire training program based upon a mental rather than physical approach to tennis.

Many athletes use mental rehearsal procedures as a means of improving their learning speed and performance. Basketball's Pete Maravich has said that he mentally replays entire games in his head. Eastern European gymnastics and diving coaches will often have their team members mentally rehearse an entire series of moves before competition as Pat McCormick, a United States diving champion, has done.

Weight lifters mentally picture their lift just before the actual attempt. When they stand in front of the bar and close their eyes they are lifting it mentally. And if they can't lift the bar mentally, then they won't be able to do it all (Schwarzenegger and Hall, 1978). Arnold Schwarzenegger uses visualization as a part of his training. "When I train the biceps, I picture huge mountains, much bigger than the biceps can ever be—just these enormous things. You do something to the mind: You fool your mind in order to do certain things. I know my biceps aren't mountains—although they may look like miniature mountains! But *thinking* that they are gets my body to respond" (Dychtwald, 1978).

The United States Olympic biathalon team has adopted mental rehearsal in preparation for their event. Deep breathing exercises are followed by a verbalization of each tiny detail of the event while they picture it mentally, and finally they review each step mentally without any verbal direction. The repetition of the mental pictures is tremendously important so they will become completely automatic. A member of the team, Lyle Nelson, first pictures the Rock of Gibraltar and then sees himself similarly steady before he sets off on his course.

Jean-Claude Killy, the United States Olympic slalom racing team, and other world class skiers use visualization to help impress on themselves the course they will be skiing. These mental dress rehearsals review every rise, hairpin, and dropoff on course; on the day of the actual race there aren't any surprises. Gallwey and Kriegel (1977) have developed an entire approach to skiing using this form of mind-body awareness.

Skeet and trapshooters have found these procedures helpful. Though they have only eight-tenths of a second to sight the target, their growing ability to concentrate their minds and bodies makes it seem as though they have plenty of time to aim and fire.

Some Soviet boxers do a ten-minute mind program before going into the ring so that they have no tensions and their nerves are ready for very rapid reactions. Young Soviet divers, who become nervous or even panicky before a diving competition, now are using mind calming to restore confidence and visualization to prompt their bodies to make the best dive.

In fact there is hardly a sport where athletes haven't attempted to use mental imagery to rehearse a performance, identify a problem, heal an injury, or learn a new technique or routine. In spite of the fairly common application of various types of imagery in sports relatively little has been done to examine scientifically the effects of these procedures. Some athletes appear to find them extremely helpful and others find them a waste of time and feel that they interfere with their performance. But failure is most likely a result of inappropriate utilization rather than an inadequacy in the procedures themselves.

A number of investigators have proposed that the use of imagery can enhance athletic performance (Corbin, 1972; Richardson, 1969; and Suinn, 1976). This involves covertly rehearsing a task with positive consequences for the specific intent of learning and has been labeled "mental practice" (Corbin, 1972). A rigorous review of the literature reported over seventy-five investigations that supported the efficacy of mental practice. While

Corbin feels that more rigorously controlled experiments are now in order he concludes that there seems to be little doubt that mental practice positively affects performance. Covert reinforcement following the imagining of the successful performance of an athletic event should enhance performance.

Imagery requires the athlete to switch focus from the physical to the mental. But in addition to the mental imagery most athletes can also recall and rehearse the kinesthetic cues (body feelings) that accompany the activity. In fact it is particularly important to be able to develop awareness of the bodily sensations that accompany a given activity if the visual and kinesthetic cues are to be recalled. The sensation of sounds and smells, from the roar of the engines in racing, the grunts and shouts in football, the quick crunch of skis in icy snow to the smell of sawdust, rosin, and popcorn, can be recreated mentally.

BENEFITS OF MENTAL IMAGERY FOR ATHLETES

Through the regular use of imagery, visualization, and rehearsal, the following results can and have been obtained:

1. Imagery and visualization develop the necessary level of *competitive tension*. Those athletes who need to psych themselves up visualize themselves in and rehearse the competitive situation; those who need to relax (decrease tension and stress) imagine some peaceful and calming scene.

2. Imagery *physically* improves precision of movement, economizes energy expenditure, and controls posture. According to French doctors Boon, Davion, and Macquet (1976), *psychological* mind training improves concentration and attention and enhances perception. It improves rapport with teammates and coaches. After competitions medical tests showed speeded-up recuperation, permitting athletes to run and perform in repeated trials. Relief from pain and muscle contraction caused by exertion was also reported.

3. Visualization increases awareness of body position and movement through rehearsal for divers, swimmers, and gymnasts.

4. Use of imagery increases performance (bowling scores increase; golf scores drop; amount of weight bench pressed increases). The process also helps to find flaws and isolate mistakes.

5. Visualization and mental rehearsal improve speed and quality of learning simple and complex motor skills. One study found that mental practice at shooting free throws was as effective as actual practice in improving performance.

6. Use of imagery increases awareness; restores energy (a process used by the Soviets and East Germans called psychic self-regulation); increases understanding and modification of memories, images of the body, and body density; and promotes recovery and relaxation.

7. Visualization increases self-discovery and helps to make changes in other areas of life.

8. Mental rehearsal keeps motivation high and helps sustain zest for training and daily practice.

9. Use of imagery eases anxieties or psychological blocks, such as fear of failure or injury, nervousness, lack of concentration, anger at teammates, decline in performance when an opponent gets ahead.

10. Visualization enables memory increase for large amounts of information necessary in most sports. This occurs because the mind sees in images and not in details (Nideffer, 1976).

11. Mental rehearsal prevents injuries, enhances the immune system, effects motivation for healthy recovery, expedites the healing process of injuries.

12. Use of imagery heightens enjoyment of activity.

13. Visualization decreases fear. Most fear comes from a feeling of no control.

14. Use of imagery changes beliefs and attitudes as symbols and images are modified.

15. Mental rehearsal allows accurate analysis of the technical aspects of performance; it teaches cues and where to focus during the athletic contest.

16. Visualization enables escape from uncomfortable situations and distracts one from anxiety-producing situations.

17. Visualization provides a tool to promote self-awareness and understanding.

18. Use of imagery aids in self-regulation, self-assessment, self-control, and biofeedback.

19. Mental rehearsal offers a vehicle to tap new energy sources.

THE MENTAL IMAGERY PROCESS

According to sports psychologist Thomas Tutko, "mental rehearsal is not Walter Mitty daydreaming. It is a drill that calls for precision and puts you to work in setting correct moves and strategies firmly in your athletic experience" (1976, p. 144).

Athletes begin the process by forming an image: a clear, mental statement of what they want to have happen. And, by repeating the statement, they soon come to expect that the desired event will indeed occur. As a result of this positive expectation the athletes begin to act in ways that will achieve the desired result and, in reality, help to bring it about. (This is similar to the self-fulfilling prophecy.) A golfer, for instance, would visualize a beautiful golf swing with the golf ball going to the desired place.

The instructions you give yourself are presented in images, for whenever you learn a sport's skill in words (from a book or somebody's explanations), you have to translate it into images for your body. The more vivid and detailed the image, the better the body can understand. This is a reason why watching someone playing well can improve the quality of your own performance.

As you rehearse an athletic activity your muscles will subtly respond to your thoughts during a game and simulate the motions just below the threshold of action, usually at a level of which you are unaware. Mental patterns initiate responses like motor responses that create easier, quicker, and more accurate, effective learning.

If you simply go through the motions in your mind you'll induce a training effect. An electromyograph placed on the involved muscle shows its tiny signal of activity. Faint contractile changes take place that are rehearsing the actual movement. The mechanism of mental practice is probably a modification of neuromuscular coordination. Even if you perceive no movement you're actually learning by doing (Morehouse and Gross, 1977, pp. 129–30).

Research by Soviets indicates that athletes during competition think in terms of images rather than words. This ability to use images and recognize particular situations enhances response and is facilitated by rehearsal. In developing the ability to visualize situations you'll find that you can more easily commit them to memory. Instead of memorizing a group of impressions and then using these to build a picture, you visualize the whole and then focus the picture to remember the parts. This strategy is effective in any situation dealing with a great deal of information that doesn't need to be processed to be remembered. As you have observed similar situations in the past and know what is contained within them, the need to catalog the elements is eliminated. If you quickly glance at a baseball diamond, for example, and someone then asks you to recall the positions of the players, you can probably do it quite easily—you process only the information that's out of place. Instead of memorizing the positions of nine defensive ball players and the offensive hitter, you notice only the one or two people out of position. Your knowledge of baseball automatically allows you to fill in the rest of the positions without having to attend to them consciously (Nideffer, 1976, p. 192).

When you engage in mental practice you rehearse your entire performance. When you play at game speed you create a real environment. If you're playing golf imagine smells, tension level, sounds, tastes, tactile impressions, form, and movement. Include your practice swing as well as your "waggle" as you address the ball. The waggle gets your signals started; if you were to leave it out, the same muscle sense of the position of the club and postural preparation of your body would be absent.

Play a perfect game of golf in mental practice—perfect, that is, for you. If you're the kind of golfer who gets at least a couple of pars on every round, your mental practice should par or birdie almost every hole. If you're not capable of hitting your best shot more than 200 yards, don't do so in mental practice. Drive to where your ball would be within the limits of the game. What will make the difference is that each shot will be your best possible effort.

A person who fears losing a sports match or visualizes a poor shot has a mental image of failure. The more the will tries to struggle with this image, the more energy the image gains. "The fatal attraction of the bunker for the nervous golfer is due to this same cause," says Émile Coué. "With his mind's eye, he sees his ball alighting in the most unfavorable spot. He may use any club he likes, he may make a long drive or a short; as long as the thought of the bunker dominates his mind, the ball will inevitably find its way towards it. The more he calls on his will to help him, the worse his plight is likely to be." Our imagery can work for or against us. It is most effective when centered.

You should always visualize a result as being perfect before you make the attempt. At the top of a ski slope imagine yourself going down the slope, rotating the turns, mogul by mogul. Feel the rhythm with which you're going to accomplish the desired run. Visualizing in this manner will refine your coordination, giving it a directness and sureness. The body follows the mind's suggestions: The entire motor nervous system is geared to a whole visual signal—"visual" meaning not just what you see but what you conceptualize as well. Use centering to visualize the result you want and your body will do its best to comply.

Centered imagery is a whole-body phenomenon, a sense of awareness—of your position on a court or field, of the position of your opponent, of your movements and the movement of equipment. This envisioning concept organizes the nervous system to make the muscles respond in a coordinated way to accomplish objectives. If you lack an image of what you want to do your muscles can't organize in the best manner available to you. Just as artists or sculptors have an image of what they want to put on canvas or a block of stone before they start brushing or chipping away, so the athlete needs to know what results are desired before movement.

As basic skills are learned and become more reflexive, some of the cues that were important earlier no longer need to be attended to consciously. Children just learning to play baseball need to pay conscious attention to the placement of their feet in the batter's box, to their grip on the bat, to their stance, to the position of their bodies, and so forth. Experienced hitters automatically assume a batting stance, and it simply feels right. They don't have to check their grip on the bat or other physical details; a total feeling exists, and once this centered feeling has developed, attention processes are freed to focus on other things. Experienced squash players, for example, don't have to wait to see the ball in flight to react. Like ranked prizefighters or open-field tacklers, they have acquired the ability to anticipate their opponent's movements (Nideffer, 1974, p. 193).

There are cues that will tell you what your opponent will do and yet many times you cannot identify what they are. If you do not know how to react to these at either a conscious or unconscious level and can't make the discriminative cue analysis, chances are you will remain very much the average athlete. This process can be enhanced through imagery training. It is a part of the way that Maury Wills and Lou Brock established the baseball record for stolen bases.

The key to effective imagery is the centering that precedes it. The visualization then is not just visceral but can be auditory, emotional, and muscular as well. The following is an effective four-step process.

1. Before beginning imagery work you need to consider the purpose of the technique and outline of the general content. This information helps to enhance performance and enjoyment.

2. Begin by centering. This may be accomplished by focusing attention on a symbol or series of mental images designed to calm the mind or a series of instructions in the mind to relax the body.

3. With eyes closed either create your own imagery as in the rehearsal technique or listen to someone (live or on tape) recite a script to create visual scenes in your mind. The scripts are designed to meet the specific needs of the athlete.

4. Practice.

TYPES OF MENTAL IMAGERY

Mental imagery can be used in a variety of forms; fantasies, progressive relaxation, guided fantasies, autogenic training, affirmations, progressive and receptive visualizations.

Mental imagery refers to the active rather than the receptive mode. Images in the receptive mode are those that "just appear" while those in the active are "made up." It is important for the athlete to do exercises and work in both modes.

Notice what form your imagery takes. Is it mainly auditory, visual, or kinesthetic? Are you more aware of motion, form, color, texture, people, objects, or abstractions? Is your imagery flat, appearing as if it were projected on a screen, or is it three-dimensional? Are you involved in the scene as a participant or are you simply an observer? (Vaughan, 1979, p. 95).

Imagery needs to be tailored for each athlete. Not only do people differ in their response to various imaginary situations, but there are countless variations of body reactions as well. When a person is confronted by images, statements, and imaginary situations, that individual is the only person in the world to "see and feel" them that particular way.

Knowing about imagery, visualization, and mental rehearsal is not going to have an impact upon you and your performance unless you practice and work with them regularly. Read the following section and do some of the procedures. Then think about them and evaluate their effectiveness and impact upon you. Use an open mind, allow time for results, and accept what you get.

Begin this process with the willingness to experience yourself fully. It is a willingness to feel your full aliveness, to be the very best you can be, to realize your unique and beautiful potential. It is willingness above all to be happy (Bry, 1978, p. 14).

Note: Images will become clearer with practice and will cease to fade so rapidly.

CENTERED IMAGERY EXERCISES

Centered Imagery to Heighten Awareness: A Beginning Process

The centered athlete knows the appropriate setting in which to feel that comfortable balanced feeling. A good way to begin centered imagery is to visualize something fairly concrete in which memory and imagination may easily be combined. The following exercise gives you an opportunity to exercise your imagination within a fairly structured setting.

Imagine an arena (stadium, court, field, track) that you are about to enter. Observe its exterior. Notice the entrance. Enter your arena and explore. See what the surface material is like, and notice the windows and doors. Travel throughout and know it all. Find high points and lows. Are there any people present? What changes would you make in this imaginary place?

In trying this particular imagery exercise some athletes visit an actual sports arena they have known rather than an imaginary one. Others create very realistic images, while a few individuals create fantasy structures that have no resemblance to their actual counterparts. There is no right way to imagine such a setting. Whatever imagery emerges for you is what you have to work with. In accepting the imagery that occurs you will learn to trust your intuitive sense of its meaning; while interpretation of imagery is a rational function, it also involves intuitive capabilities.

Changing Places and Faces

This procedure enhances the centered imagery process. Practice allows the athlete to develop images that can improve performance and heighten awareness and appreciation. Many runners use this process to visualize themselves as animals and begin to move as horses, cheetahs, deer, greyhounds, or antelope.

Sit comfortably, close your eyes, and take a few minutes to

become quiet and centered. Become aware of your breathing and notice any physical sensations that are present for you at this moment. Be aware of your feelings and notice the thoughts that are going through your mind. Be aware of how it feels to be you at this moment.

(One-minute pause)

Separate yourself from the immediate surroundings and imagine yourself in a completely different environment. Picture a pleasant and natural surrounding. Concentrate on the first place that comes to mind, and when it begins to fade go to another.

(Pause for one to two minutes)

Now imagine that you are a different being—a person or animal. Move from setting to setting as this new form.

(Pause for one to two minutes)

Take a deep breath and return to the immediate setting. Move your arms and legs and when you are ready open your eyes.

Centering Statements

Sit in a comfortable position. Close your eyes. Be aware of the center of your body as you take ten breaths. Choose one of the following centering statements and repeat very slowly eight to ten times. This process can be repeated daily until it becomes unimportant. Then choose or develop another.

I am calmer every day.

Every day and every way I am running faster and smoother.

I am stronger every day.

I am clearer every day.

I have more energy each day.

I learn from everything.

I feel at one with the earth, flowers, trees, sun, grass, clouds, wind, rain, sky, and stars.

I gain deep satisfaction from _____ (running, swimming, tennis, or whatever).

I am safe and happy.

I am light and floating.

It is more important that I please myself than please others.

This is the moment where preparation and opportunity meet.

I radiate love to all people.

Use it or lose it.

Hills are my friends.

Centered Imagery to Neutralize Opponents

Athletes often are upset or distracted by their opponents or other competitors. The following process can be used to help ease this influence.

Close your eyes. Center yourself. Take ten centering breaths. Visualize your opponent. Once the image is clear repeat, "My opponent is not important: Calm and confident I play well." Repeat this mantra 15 times each day.

Centered Rehearsal: The Entire Game

This process allows the centered athlete to practice and rehearse anywhere. Research supports centered rehearsal as a way to improve both performance and enjoyment. This is best done before a workout or contest.

Find a quiet place. Close your eyes. Center yourself. Take ten centering breaths. Picture yourself at the site of your event or workout. Notice the clothes you are wearing, the temperature, the lighting, and the surroundings. Imagine yourself happy, relaxed, and confident. Visualize your game or event from start to finish.

Picture yourself performing at your finest with power, ease, and confidence. Pay attention to crowd reactions, physical feelings, breathing, and muscle tension. Feel the exhilaration of knowing you have done your best. Seeing yourself in a centered and balanced state throughout will increase your success and pleasure.

Centered Rehearsal: Special Skills

This procedure helps to strengthen any aspect of your game or sport.

Close your eyes. Center yourself. Take ten centering breaths. Visualize a specific play such as a double play, tennis serve, running race start, or free throw. Imagine you are performing this action properly. Practice the action in slow motion three times. Go slowly enough so that each detail can be observed. Practice at the actual game speed five times.

Centered Imagery to Remove Tension

Move slowly down your body—jaw, neck, shoulders, back, upper and lower arms, hands, chest, abdomen, thighs, calves, ankles, feet—until every part of your body is more relaxed. For each part of the body mentally picture the tension, then picture it melting away like ice or snow in the spring, leaving centeredness.

Centered Imagery: Create Your Own

Athletic performance and enjoyment depend largely upon focusing one's attention, whether on the field in which it happens, on one's teammates and opponents, on the ball, or on the functioning of one's own body. Success depends in large part on the steadiness and clarity of the players' concentration. The practices we have advocated in this section help improve both performance and enjoyment in athletics because they help bring us to a deeper center, a truer and more effective level of personal functioning.

Centered imagery activities can be created to work with all aspects of the athlete's performance. We urge you to develop your own processes around themes such as the following (please let us know of your "developments"):

- speed
- smooth and flowing motion
- movement as one with your opponent, tapping the same energy source
- endurance and stamina
- flying or jumping
- oneness with the ball, paddle, or other equipment
- slowing down the game to deal better with its subtleties.

REFERENCES

ACHTERBERG, J. AND LAWLIS, G. F. *Imagery of cancer*. Champaign, IL: Institute for Personality and Ability Testing, 1978.

BENSON, H. *The mind/body effect*. New York: Morrow, 1978.

BLOOMFIELD, H. AND KORY, R. *The holistic way to health and happiness*. New York: Simon & Schuster, 1978.

BOON, H., DAVION, Y. AND MACQUET, J. C. *LaSophrologie: Une Révolution en psychologia, pédagogie, médicine?* Paris: Retz, 1976.

BROWN, B. *New mind, new body*. New York: Harper and Row, 1975.

BROWN, B. *Stress and the art of biofeedback*. New York: Harper and Row, 1977.

BRY, A. *Directing the movies of your mind*. New York: Harper and Row, 1978.

CORBIN, E. B. In W. P. Morgan (ed.) *Erogenic aids and muscular performance*. New York: Academic Press, 1972.

COUSINS, N. *Anatomy of an illness*. New York: W. W. Norton, 1979.

DYCHTWALD, K. *Bodymind*. New York: Pantheon, 1976.

DYCHTWALD, K. The powers of mind: A New Age interview with Arnold Schwarzenegger. *New Age*, 1978, 3 (8), 38–43+.

GALLWEY, W. T. *The inner game of tennis.* New York: Random House, 1974.

GALLWEY, T. AND KRIEGEL, B. *Inner skiing.* New York: Random House, 1977.

JACOBSEN, E. *Progressive relaxation.* Chicago: University of Chicago Press, 1942.

KHATENA, J. Vividness of imagery and creative self-perception. *The Gifted Child Quarterly,* 1975, 19 (1), 33–37.

KOPP, S. B. *If you meet the buddha on the road, kill him.* Palo Alto, CA: Science and Behavior Books, 1972.

LEONARD, G.B. *The ultimate athlete.* New York: Viking Press, 1974.

LUTHE, W. *Autogenic therapy. Vol. I–VI.* New York: Grune and Stratton, 1969.

McCLUGGAGE, D. *The centered skier.* Vermont Crossroads: Vermont Crossroads Press, 1977.

MILLMAN, D. *Whole body fitness: Training mind, body, and spirit.* New York: Clarkson N. Potter, 1979.

MOREHOUSE, L. E. AND GROSS, L. *Maximum performance.* New York: Simon & Schuster, 1977.

MURPHY, M. *Golf in the kingdom.* New York: Viking Press, 1972.

MURPHY, M. AND WHITE, R. B. *The psychic side of sports.* Reading, MA: Addison and Wesley, 1978.

NIDEFFER, R. *The inner athlete: Mind plus muscle for winning.* New York: T. Y. Crowell, 1974.

OSTRANDER, S., SCHROEDER, L. AND OSTRANDER, N. *Super-learning.* New York: Delacorte, 1979.

OYLE, I. *The new American medicine show.* Santa Cruz: Unity Press, 1979.

PELLETIER, K. R. *Holistic medicine: From stress to optimum health.* New York: Delacorte, 1979.

RICHARDSON, A. *Mental imagery.* New York: Springer, 1969.

ROHE, F. *The zen of running.* New York: Random House, 1974.

SCHWARZENEGGER, A. AND HALL, D. K. *Arnold: The education of a bodybuilder.* New York: Simon & Schuster, 1977.

SHEALY, C. N. *90 days to self-health.* New York: Bantam, 1977.

SIMONTON, O. C., MATTHEWS-SIMONTON, S. AND CREIGHTON, J. *Getting well again.* Los Angeles: J. P. Tarcher, 1978.

SPINO, M. *Beyond jogging: The innerspaces of running.* Millbrae, CA: Celestial Arts, 1976.

SPINO, M. *Running home: The body/mind fitness book.* Millbrae, CA: Celestial Arts, 1977.

SPINO, M. AND WARREN, J. E. *Mike Spino's mind/body running program.* New York: Bantam, 1979.

SUINN, R. M. Body thinking for Olympic champs. *Psychology Today*, 1976, 10, 38–43.

TUTKO, T. AND TOSI, U. *Sports psyching: Playing your best game all of the time.* Los Angeles: J. P. Tarcher, 1976.

VAUGHAN, F. E. *Awakening intuition.* Garden City: Anchor Press/Doubleday, 1979.

3

Body expansion: stretching exercises for all sports

No matter what your spiritual condition is, no matter where you find yourself in the universe, your choice is always the same: to expand your awareness or contract it. *

Most athletes have never learned how to take care of themselves. They lack physical education. Any athlete has strength and skills; great, centered athletes seem to expand beyond these characteristics and have movements that are effortless, graceful, catlike. The centered athlete is physically more adaptable to game situations and is able to change direction more quickly and easily. There is less chance of injury as the athlete learns the ability to fall properly or absorb a blow more easily. Finally, the centered athlete knows the moments to be totally relaxed when at play.

HOW THE BODY WORKS

There are more than five hundred muscles and more than two hundred bones in the human body. Bones are the basic framework of the body. Some, such as the skull, chest, and ribs serve primarily a protective function. And others, like the vertebral column, which encases the spinal cord and supports the back, are both protective and supportive. Muscles are concerned mainly with movements.

Muscles attach to bones, connected by tendons. Tendons are not elastic and are more easily torn, often away from the bone.

*Reprinted by permission of the author from *The Lazy Man's Guide to Enlightenment* by Thaddeus Golas.

Muscle tissue is elastic and lengthens and shortens. Bones fit together at joints, bound together by these same muscles. Muscle movement can be voluntary or involuntary, but muscles never relax completely when, say, binding a joint to its mate. Muscles can be strengthened, bones cannot.

The heart is a muscle, the lungs are not. The lungs depend upon the contraction and retraction of the muscles of the rib cage and diaphragm for the capacity of air they can exchange. The air we breathe is the oxygen we need. It burns up the foodstuffs we have eaten to provide fuel for the body in the form of energy.

As we inhale air into our lungs the oxygen is removed, forced into tiny, and balloonlike red blood cells and sent through our bloodstream to the heart, where it is pumped throughout the entire system to the muscles, nerves, and other tissues that feed from it. The oxygen replaces carbon dioxide wastes, the red blood cells return through the bloodstream to the lungs where the carbon dioxide is exhaled, and the now empty cells receive a fresh supply of oxygen. The cycle is complete. This is a simplified look at the complicated process, and it is all that the nonprofessional athlete needs to know. The goal of expansion is to increase the ability of the body to perform physical acts more freely and easily.

Bodily movement of any kind depends on the ability of muscles to move the joints in the manner the brain dictates. Muscles and joints that have a full and proper range of movement improve the quality of movement. They coordinate flexibility with strength and power.

Expansion procedures will allow the athlete to surpass what were once thought to be unalterable limits.

An athlete who concentrates on a single sport or exercise will strengthen some muscles, overdevelop others, and weaken (tighten, shorten, stress, traumatize) others. Aches, pains, injuries, and stiff bodies are almost inevitable.

Expansion procedures are not calisthenics. Calisthenics are dull, of questionable value, possibly harmful, and no fun. Body expansion procedures do not involve the strain, pain, sudden movement, extension, or repetition of calisthenics. These are procedures that restore balance, integration, and flow to the athlete. They help muscles learn to work together in a way that allows the athlete to reach the best possible condition. This involves learning to move the entire body as economically as possible through breath control and flexibility of motion. The stress is on developing elasticity through patience, concentration, and control.

Body expansion is a centering tool as well. Many words express the feeling of being completely expanded: total awareness, completeness, freedom, love, ecstasy, certainty, stability, supreme intelligence, compassion. The expansion process consists of a series of basic and advanced stretching exercises that expand the athlete in the following ways:

1. *Muscle capacity* is increased by dissolving tension. This increased strength provides the foundation for movement. Expanding yields a continued and improved performance level.

2. *Range of movement* is increased as old body patterns and rigid habits of movement that decrease the ability to move freely and spontaneously are dissolved. Expanding helps one enjoy movement and experience a loose, floating feeling of weightlessness. Specific expansion procedures will focus on the actual musculature movements of each athletic event. They help the nervous system control movement. A healthy and limber body moves freely and easily.

3. *Timing and balance* are improved as athletes gain more control and understanding of themselves. Athletes naturally learn more about the proper techniques of individual movement because mind and body learn to concentrate on rhythms and paces and become less concerned with ego. When the ego is not involved learning and understanding take place without interference through natural awareness of personal development. Expanding helps athletes to work on rhythms when exercising as it makes for a feeling of well-being. Athletes appreciate movement and its benefits more with expanding because it helps to make regularity with exercise possible. The expansion process also helps athletes learn to understand fully the uniqueness of their individual physical-mental being with their own comfortable and enjoyable rhythms. If athletes do not learn and develop rhythm, they lose improvement and enjoyment.

4. *Enjoyment and pleasure* increase as athletes gently stretch away the forces that cause uptightness. Good feelings are developed. As we grow older we become even more inflexible, and as the body becomes tighter the mind becomes more closed to new understandings. Expand your body and your mind will follow. Expand to feel good and not just to look different or to become inflexible. Expanding will help you most if you work toward good feelings. Expanding will help you to become supple, graceful, and optimally healthy. Not only will these procedures facilitate athletic performance and development, but you will begin to enjoy the feelings of pleasure and satisfaction that emerge from their mindful and regular practice.

5. *Endurance* is increased as practice sessions leave one elevated and revitalized rather than tired and drained. Economical motions are developed that require minimum rather than maximum effort. The activities that initially left you aching and breathless will become virtually effortless.

6. *Flexibility and muscle rejuvenation* are increased by expansion, which releases tensions, leading to muscle relaxation. The increase in flexibility allows athletes to move with greater ease and therefore improved performance. The stretches are designed to *lengthen* muscles, elasticize tendons and ligaments, and facilitate the development of a healthy, supple, integrated, relaxed body. Stiffness can and does develop over months and years. We need to allow time for regular and moderate activity to wear this away. Tightness is a feeling that limits the enjoyment of movement and the development of personal potential. Tightness and tension are not a problem when expanding is done properly and regularly.

7. *Immunity to injuries* comes from general expansion procedures. They also help to prevent muscle soreness and stiffness and increase the overall capacity to move freely. It is important to be aware that athletic injuries can be reduced through increased flexibility. When there is greater movement range within the joints the ligaments and other tissues

are not easily torn or stretched. Increased flexibility also aids the body in reducing the shock of impact in contact sports and provides athletes greater freedom of movement in all directions. Most college and professional teams as well as Olympic athletes use this process to reduce or rehabilitate injuries.

8. *Stress and tension in muscles* are reduced by expansion. Muscular tension results from conflict between body and mind, from the interaction between athletes and their environment, and from the internal conflict between athletes' standards of performance and how they actually perform. Our normal experiences cause unrecognized tension and stress that can be significantly reduced through stretching exercises.

WHO SHOULD USE EXPANSION PROCEDURES   Everyone can learn and benefit from expansion, and it is tremendously important to realize that everyone is capable of expansion. There is no sense of comparison in it, no conflict of how you think you should look when doing expansion procedures. No specific physical skills are necessary for this development, other than learning to be centered. We can all tap more of our latent potential. People actually learn to love expansion.

WHEN TO PRACTICE EXPANSION PROCEDURES   Expansion can be done any time that you feel like it. You can stretch while waiting for breakfast, dinner, or a bus. You may do it at work, in a car, walking down the road, under a nice shady tree after a hike, or at the beach. When a part of your body feels tense or sore, move it gently around, extend it: loosen it up. It's that easy. Expansion needs to be done before or after physical activity, when the body and mind are full of tension, after sitting or standing for a period of time, before and after sleep, and after rest.

Jim Fixx in The Complete Book of Running (1977) describes a UCLA study where healthy men ran on fast treadmills without warming up and were found to have abnormal ECGs (electrocardiograms) indicating insufficient blood supply to the heart; two minutes of warming up, however, resulted in markedly reduced ECG abnormalities. Gentle stretching will help wake up your body, step up the activity of the cardiovascular system, and prepare muscles for work.

Once you learn expansion you will see that it is possible to expand many different muscles at almost any phase or time. You will develop your own routines to suit your particular needs at any given time. If you want to expand and it feels good, then do it. Don't let your mind create reasons why you should not. Have an open mind. Move and expand by how you feel (Anderson, 1975, p. 11).

Pick a time of day when you are likely to be bothered least. Experiment with different times of the day, then stay with the most comfortable. The morning is the hardest for many people, since their bodies are stiff from sleep—but it helps the day begin from a centered point. Others prefer expanding after work or workouts to relieve tensions and feel refreshed.

Recent research (Roth and Benjamin, 1979) indicates that warming up muscles and lubricating joints will increase the benefits of expanding. "A warmup means actually heating up the body by pumping blood into the muscles. The easy movement of light stretch exercises necessary to do this will also produce synovial fluid for the joints and wake up the body's nervous system for better coordination. . . . A cold muscle can be compared to a dry sponge. Trying to stretch it is nearly futile and might even tear some fibres. A warm muscle, full of freshly pumped blood, can be compared with a wet sponge, providing more flexibility and suppleness than any cold dry stretch can give" (pp. 15–16).

WHERE SHOULD ONE PRACTICE EXPANSION PROCEDURES? These procedures can actually be done almost anywhere. Most athletes, however, prefer a secluded place with a rug and mat. Try different settings and discover what works for you. Dychtwald recommends the following in setting up a permanent facility:

> Select a roomy, well-ventilated area where physical and psychological distractions are at a minimum. These exercises require a flat and level surface with sufficient space to stretch your trunk and limbs without interference. It is helpful to

always practice your exercises in the same "exercise sanctuary." In this way, your exercise space can become a special place to comfortably retreat and focus on yourself. This also holds true if you intend to practice these stretches outdoors. Select a comfortable, level environment where you can pay close attention to yourself and not be distracted. Cover your practice surface with a large towel, mat or pad. Choose this covering carefully and be certain that you will feel comfortable using it with your exercise.*

How to Practice Expansion Procedures Expanding is not just a substitute for calisthenics, but it is a basic element in all activity. The process begins by centering through systematic relaxation and breathing. Concentrate on the feeling of expansion, not flexibility; stressing flexibility at the beginning will only lead to overstretching, which leads to possible injuries and a negative attitude. Expanding muscles daily is necessary and enjoyable. Learn to expand properly, within your limits, and with a good mental attitude and awareness of the pleasure and enjoyment being deserved. Disregard the myth "if it doesn't hurt, it isn't any good." Straining is not expanding. All activity is painless and easy if we just know what we can do, what we like to do, and the speed at which we can do it to get enjoyment and understanding.

The following procedures can serve as guidelines for effective expansion:

1. You are a stretching expert. You know more about precisely where, and to what degree, you need to stretch than any expert, for the body in question is *yours*. Do not compare yourself to others. There is no ladder to climb or contest to win. Some of us will be able to touch our toes, others just above the ankles. Progress at your own rate and adjust the expanding exercises to your individual needs. Remember people are different.

2. It is not important just how flexible you are, only that you are

*Reprinted from *The Jogger* with permission of the National Jogging Association.

feeling better, improving, and enjoying the process. Learn to listen to your body.

3. Regular practice is the most important factor.

4. No two days are the same. We are different every day. Sometimes we are more tight or loose than at other times.

5. Don't bounce when you stretch. Bobbing, bouncing, jerking, pushing, or pumping result in further tightening, tearing, or pulling. DeVries (1966) found that bouncing invokes the stretch *reflex*, which is the opposite to stretching. These are "ballistic" exercises and expanding involves static exercises that feature slow and rhythmic stretching, stopping, and holding a position at the first point of discomfort.

6. Do what works for you. Because we are all in different shape and shapes, each person will respond to the procedures differently and create an individual way of performing.

7. Take your time. Results of expansion are both immediate and long range. By gradually working within your own comfortable and painless limits you will be able to go beyond your present limits and come closer to your potentials.

8. Centering is the key to expanding. It needs to be done with no outside pressure and with mental alertness. The thoughts, beliefs, and feelings that create tension and tightness need to be dissolved.

9. The link between body and mind is breath. Breathing connects us with our environment. Through breathing we feel our environment physically and psychically. The amount of energy available for the functioning of our brain and all the rest of our body is directly proportionate to the amount of air in our lungs, which determines the amount of oxygen available to our cells. Breathing is important. Slow and rhythmic breathing help to relax the body so that the mind can concentrate on the right "expansion" procedure. When happy, centered, and relaxed, we breathe freely. When angry, fearful, or tense, we freeze up, hold our breath, or pant in rapid, rasping gulps. As we free our breath we relax our emotions and let go

of our body tensions. Proper breathing regulates basic physiological responses. Your breathing should be slow, rhythmic, and controlled. Exhale as you are bending forward and then breathe at a slow rhythmic pace as you hold the expansion pose. Do not hold your breath. If you are not breathing properly or relaxed, you are not expanding properly.

10. Clearly visualize the procedure. Thought is a form of energy and will produce subtle changes.

11. Think of the goal of no strain and no pain. Allow your entire body to remain relaxed throughout all movement, not strained or tense.

12. Be under control. All actions should be executed in a deliberate, unhurried manner, never "quickly" or "suddenly."

13. Stay within your limits. Expanding should be done within an individual's limits with a progressive increase in the pose as the stretch lessens (the body is increasing in flexibility). If you are tight and inflexible patience and relaxation are the keys to improvement.

14. Begin when the body is warm. Expansion is easier, feels better, and does more good when you are warm. (Cold muscles hurt more and are likely to be tense.)

WHAT TO FEEL AND LOOK FOR IN EXPANSION

The expanding feeling is different from that of pain. You must learn to operate within your limits without strain or pain. It doesn't matter how far you can stretch. It's all an edge. It is only a line of demarcation. Playing at the boundaries is the most important thing. The expanding feeling lies between no strain or feeling and too much strain and pain. The feeling should be in the belly of the muscle and strenuous but without pain.

At certain areas you do not want to feel stretch. These are at, or close to, the joints where there are mostly tendons and ligaments. Tendons are like rope and hardly able to stretch at all. If you pull on them they will only become weakened. Ligaments hold bones together, and when they are stretched they cannot do the job. Having loose and wobbly joints can cause serious injuries and other problems.

The process that will yield an appropriate stretch in the correct area is as follows:

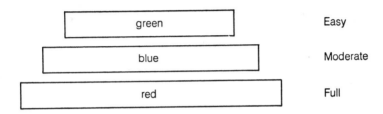

Begin with an *Easy*, gentle, and slow stretch and hold for 15 to 25 seconds; then fade into the *Moderate* range and hold for an additional 35 to 45 seconds or longer. Make sure you feel the stretch in the belly of the muscle. Do not do stretching in the *Full* range. As your flexibility increases you will need to gradually lengthen the *Moderate* range as you come closer to your potential.

This point of strain demarcates one of the many "edges" within your body and identifies a point of limited flexibility. Do not try to force yourself past this edge. Instead, remain centered at this point and hold the position while you continue breathing for the prescribed period of time. When you do this your body will respond by focusing attention on the spot. This focus encourages blood and energy to bathe the related muscles and organs, which in turn allows the muscles to relax and stretch, the joints to become more elastic, and the internal organs to function more effectively (Dychtwald, 1979).

As you increase the stretch a change in feeling will result. You should learn how to stretch by how you feel, not by forcing yourself to do something you are not ready to do. Remember that there is a *Moderate* range of stretching between the *Easy* and the *Full* stretch. A good stretch is in the area of the *Moderate* stretch (Anderson, 1975).

EXPANSION EXERCISES

Each exercise is introduced by a description of the benefit it offers—that is, the effect the exercise has upon you either immediately or after prolonged use. Next come the instructions on the exercise itself.

Do not try to copy the pictures, but use them as visual aids to give you the fundamental stretch. Then do what works for you. One's own experience is the best teacher. Use a combination of approaches and find what fits you and your system. Select a comfortable balance of forward and backward bending poses as well as a blend of twisting, rotating, arching, and inverting positions. The following sequences are possible expansion programs for different sports:

RUNNING	RACQUET SPORTS
Grounding	Wall Stretch
Bend and Hang	Shoulder Expanding
Quarter Squat	Side Bend
Bend and Hang	Pull Down
Pull Down	Wall Push
Wall Push	Grounding
Quadriceps Stretch	Bend and Hang
Hamstring Stretch	Quarter Squat
Side Bend	Bend and Hang
SWIMMING	Quadriceps Stretch
Shoulder Expanding	Hip Flexor
Side Bend	
Bend and Hang	
Quarter Squat	
Bend and Hang	
Groin Expanding	
Wall Push	

SKIING	CYCLING/BIKING
Bend and Hang	Wall Push
Quarter Squat	Grounding
Bend and Hang	Bend and Hang
Hip Flexor	Quarter Squat
Quadriceps Stretch	Bend and Hang
Grounding	Quadriceps Stretch
Wall Push	Groin Expanding
Shoulder Expanding	Pull Down
Side Bend	Neck Rotations
Bend and Hang	

Expansion Breath

BENEFITS This basic procedure helps to rebalance and center your entire system. It produces a calm feeling accompanied by heightened awareness and should precede any sequence of procedures.

INSTRUCTIONS Stand upright with the feet positioned directly below the shoulders. Bend the knees slightly. Clasp hands and slowly raise arms overhead as you inhale. The breath controls the arm movement and it will seem as if the breath is lifting the arms. Let your forearms and hands drop down behind your neck. Exhaling slowly, bring hands and forearms over your head and allow your arms to float down. (See illustration on page 46.)

Full Body Swing

BENEFITS This procedure loosens the joints before exercise and stretches the muscles in the front, back, and sides of the legs and waist.

INSTRUCTIONS Stand comfortably with your feet shoulder width

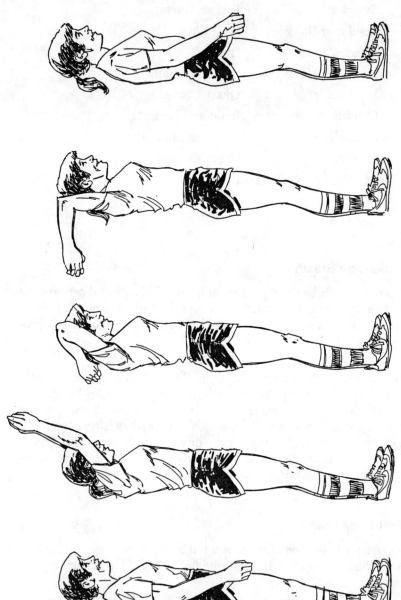

Expansion Breath

apart. Inhale and slowly raise your arms. Extend them out to either side parallel to the floor, palms down. Then swing your body all the way to the right side (include your entire body, from your ankles to your neck). When you have swung as far to the right as is comfortably possible, reverse directions and swing all the way around to the left. Find a rhythm that feels good. Breathe deeply and relax your entire body as you perform these swings. Continue swinging back and forth for a count of 25. Slow down gently and come to rest at your own speed. Then exhale and slowly lower your arms back to your sides. Complete the procedure with an expansion breath.

Full Body Swing

Quadriceps Stretch

BENEFITS   This procedure relieves stress that often accumulates in muscles surrounding the groin, pelvis, and lower back. Stretches and vitalizes muscles of the lower back and legs, especially the quadriceps and hamstrings.

INSTRUCTIONS   Keep your back straight and use one hand to keep your balance (it is permissible to hold onto or lean up against something) and the other to pull your knee toward your chest. Don't strain. Get an *Easy* stretch and then gradually increase it. (Hold for 45 seconds.) Focusing on your breathing, grab your foot from the outside with your hand. Slowly pull your foot toward your buttocks until you feel the stretch in your quadriceps. (Hold for 30 seconds.) Complete the stretch by slowly extending your lower leg into your hand and intensify the stretch in the thigh. This will straighten out your arm. (Hold for 10 seconds.) Repeat with the other leg. Place both feet firmly on the ground and finish with an expansion breath.

Quadriceps Stretch

Wall Stretch

BENEFITS   This posture rejuvenates the legs and mind. It can be used before and after activity and helps keep the legs light with plenty of consistent energy by increasing circulation.

INSTRUCTIONS   Lie on the floor with your buttocks against a wall. Elevate your feet and rest them against the wall. Close your eyes and breathe through your center. Be as still as possible and listen to the sounds of your body. (Hold for three minutes.) Return to an upright position and finish with an expansion breath.

Wall Stretch

Shoulder Expanding

BENEFITS   This procedure is used to stretch the deltoid and tricep muscles of the shoulder.

INSTRUCTIONS   Begin with both feet firmly grounded and knees slightly bent. Breathe deeply through your center for five breaths.

49

With your arms overhead, hold the elbow of one arm with the hand of the other arm. Gently pull the elbow behind your head, creating a stretch. Do it slowly. (Hold the stretch for 30 seconds.) Repeat with the other arm. Finish with an expansion breath.

Alternative: With arms extended overhead and palms together, stretch your arms upward and slightly backward. Breathe in as you stretch upward, holding the stretch for five to eight seconds.

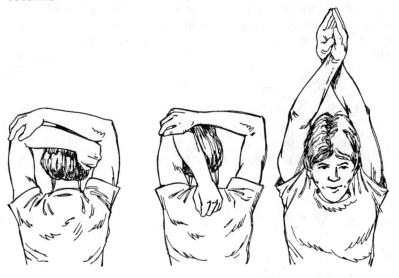

Shoulder Expanding

Pull Down

BENEFITS This procedure stretches the arms, shoulders, and spinal column.

INSTRUCTIONS Grasp a fence or ledge so that your hands are approximately an inch above shoulder height. Center yourself and spread your legs to shoulder width and move away from the fence, sufficiently to fully extend your arms in a "locked" position. Breathe easily and smoothly. The legs should be kept straight and the feet securely planted directly under the hips to offer maximum support. Keeping the arms fully extended and "locked," permitting the head to "hang" naturally, shift the weight of your body back and downward creating a pull-down effect. (Hold a comfortable stretch for 45 seconds.) Stand up and finish with an expansion breath.

Pull Down

Groin Expanding

BENEFITS   This procedure loosens up the tight muscles of the groin region.

INSTRUCTIONS   Sit firmly on the ground. Straighten out your legs and hold your toes upright. Breathe slowly until you achieve a centered balance. Rotate your hips in a forward direction as you slowly bend forward to stretch. Be sure to keep your back straight. If possible, use your hands out in front of you for balance. (Hold the stretch where you can relax for 60 seconds.) This is a difficult way to stretch for many athletes. These muscles need time to loosen up, so be patient. Remain seated and finish with an expansion breath.

Groin Expanding

Ankle Stretch

BENEFITS This procedure stretches the Achilles tendon, ankle, and calves.

INSTRUCTIONS Stand with your toes on a stairstep or a telephone book, heels over the edge. Lower the heels below the toes and hold for a count of ten. Release, rest a few seconds, and repeat until your calf muscles are tired. Do not go too fast. Go slow and work on centering. You may initially need to hold onto the stair railing or a car for balance. The leg of the Achilles tendon and ankle being stretched should be kept straight. Stretch in the *Easy* phase. Place both feet firmly on the ground and finish with an expansion breath.

Ankle Stretch

Wall Push

BENEFITS   This procedure is designed to stimulate the calf, Achilles tendon, and ankle.

INSTRUCTIONS   Face a fence, wall, or something to lean on. Stand a little way from this support and rest your forearms on it with your forehead on the back of your hands. Breathe deeply through your center for ten breaths. Now bend one knee and bring that knee toward the wall. Keep your other leg straight and heel down as you move your hips slightly toward the wall. Keep your toes pointed and straight ahead. This stretch should be felt in the middle of the calf of the straight leg. (Hold this for one minute.) Repeat process with the other leg. If you feel it behind the knee or at the Achilles, bend your knee slightly. Place both feet firmly on the ground and finish with an expansion breath.

Wall Push

Hamstring Stretch

Hamstring Stretch

BENEFITS   This procedure lengthens muscles in the back of the body, particularly the hamstrings, quadriceps, and the lower back.

INSTRUCTIONS   Choose something near you like a tree, or a fence, or table, or large rock that is about waist high or at a height from which you can comfortably stretch. Place the back of your heel on the object and keep your leg straight. You want to keep the leg that is raised straight, so don't try to use something that is too high. Find a place that is fairly comfortable. Your other leg, on the ground, should be nearly straight, with your foot pointed in a proper walking or running position. Breathe in through your nose and exhale through your mouth. Breathe away all tension. (Ten breaths.) Now that you are centered, slowly bend forward at the waist until you feel a good stretch in the back of the raised leg. Hold and relax. Find the *Easy* stretch, relax, and then stretch further when it becomes easier with the other leg. Place both feet firmly on the ground and finish with an expansion breath.

Hamstring Stretch

Bend and Hang

BENEFITS This procedure stretches the hamstrings and abductor muscles. It helps to keep the legs fit, and the abdomen and lower back stress free.

INSTRUCTIONS Start in a standing position, feet about shoulder width apart. Breathe through your center until you feel grounded. Slowly bend forward at the waist and let your neck and arms relax. Go to the point where you feel a slight stretch in the back of your legs. Stretch in this *Easy* phase for 25 seconds, until you are relaxed. By concentrating mentally on the area being expanded and relaxing, you will feel less of a stretch. From this *Easy* phase go into the *Moderate* phase of stretching and hold for at least as long as you did the *Easy* phase. Stand upright and finish with an expansion breath.

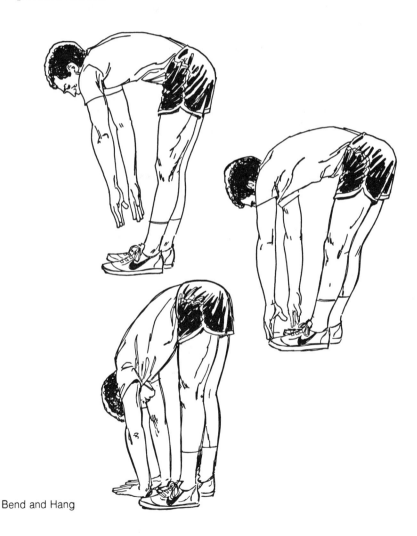

Bend and Hang

Quarter Squat

BENEFITS This procedure contracts the quadriceps and relaxes the hamstrings. Note: This is a good procedure to use after the "Bend and Hang" because it blocks the stretch reflex and allows the muscles to stretch and expand to their maximum without pain. This occurs because these muscles do opposite actions— quadriceps are flexors and the hamstrings are extensors, and these muscles are of the same mass.

INSTRUCTIONS Assume a quarter-squat position with your heels flat, toes pointed straight ahead and feet about shoulder width apart. Breathe in slowly and deeply, filling the abdomen first and then the lungs. Exhale, emptying the lungs and then the abdomen. Concentrate on your centering and realize how solid you have become. (Hold this position for one minute.) Stand upright and finish with an expansion breath.

Quarter Squat

Grounding

Grounding

BENEFITS   This procedure stretches from the front part of the lower legs, the knees, back, ankles, Achilles tendons, and deep groin.

INSTRUCTIONS   From a standing position, squat down with your feet flat and toes pointed out at approximately 45-degree angles. Your heels should be 4 to 12 inches apart, depending on how loose you are or, as you become familiar with stretching, depend-

59

ing on exactly what parts of your body you want to stretch. At first you may have a problem with balance—falling backward because of tight ankles and Achilles tendons. If you are unable to squat as shown you could hold onto an object or rest against it. (Hold for 60 seconds.) Stand upright and finish with an expansion breath.

Hip Flexor

BENEFITS This procedure is used to stretch the muscles of the entire groin and hip areas. Increased flexibility in the muscles of hip flexion and extension will allow for an increased stride and thereby increase running speed.

INSTRUCTIONS The initial posture is similar to positioning oneself in "starting blocks" for a footrace. The right leg is extended to the rear, with the right knee resting on the ground and the left foot placed directly under the chest. Be certain to keep the left heel on the ground. Breathe deeply, and slowly shift your body weight forward until you feel sufficient stretch of the muscles of hip flexion. (Hold this position for 60 seconds.) Switch legs and repeat the process. Return to an upright position and finish with an expansion breath.

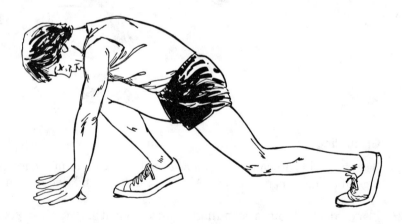

Hip Flexor

Side Bend

BENEFITS   This procedure stretches the muscles on the inside and outside of the legs.

INSTRUCTIONS   Stand with your feet about shoulder width apart and toes pointed slightly outward. Keeping your legs fairly straight, place one hand on your hip for support while you extend your other arm up and over your head. Now slowly bend to the side of the hand on the hip. Move slowly. Feel a good stretch. (Hold the stretch for 20 seconds and relax.) Remain centered and always come out of a stretch slowly and under control. No quick movements or jerks. Complete the procedure with an expansion breath.

Side Bend

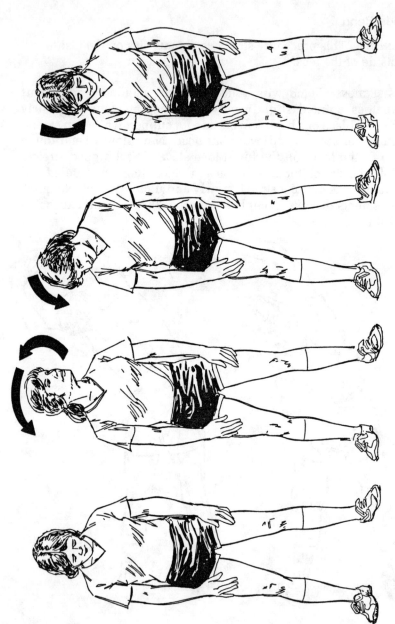

Neck Rotations

Neck Rotations

BENEFITS This procedure restores flexibility and elasticity to the muscles of the throat and neck.

INSTRUCTIONS Stand in a comfortable position. Center yourself. *Very slowly* roll your head back around in a full circle as you keep your back straight. While you are rolling your head around slowly you may feel that you should hold or stop at a certain place that feels tight. Do so, but do not strain. If you are holding a position relax and concentrate on your breathing and it will gradually loosen up. Most people experience some grinding noises or crackling sounds in the neck when they first begin to do neck rotations. This is normal. (Do six rotations in each direction.) Finish with an expansion breath.

REFERENCES

ANDERSON, B. *Stretching*. (New York: Random House/Shelter Publications, 1980).

DeVRIES, H. A. *Physiology of exercise for physical education and athletes*. Dubuque, IA: Wm. C. Brown, 1966.

DYCHTWALD, K. Bodymind stretching for runners. *Jogger*, December/January, 1979/1980.

FALLS, H. B., WALLIS, E. L. AND LOGAN, G. A. *Foundations of conditioning*. New York: Academic Press, 1970.

FIXX, J. *The complete book of running*. New York: Random House, 1977.

GOLAS, T. *The lazy man's guide to enlightenment*. New York: Bantam Books, 1980.

JACKSON, I. *Yoga and the athlete*. Mountain View, CA: World Publications, 1975.

MILLMAN, D. *Whole body fitness: Training mind, body and spirit*. New York: Clarkson N. Potter, 1979.

ROTH, P. AND BENJAMIN, B. Warming up vs. stretching. *Running News*, November, 1979.

63

4

Experiments
in centered running

Running is the finest cardiovascular fitness and conditioning activity. It has become the standard against which all other exercises are measured. Running stresses the heart and lungs more than almost any other athletic event. While running the heart rate rises and remains elevated, rather than fluctuating up and down as it does in tennis, baseball, and basketball. Cycling and swimming are similar to running in this regard. This continuous, rather than intermittent, stress is exceedingly beneficial to the heart.

The President's Council on Physical Fitness and Sports asked seven experts for their opinions on how different sports rate in promoting physical fitness. The results showed running at the top of the list of 14 sports, not only in respect to cardiovascular endurance but also in terms of total health benefits.

Running is both a sport and an exercise. Some of the major advantages of running are:

1. It is healthy for the body *and* mind.

2. It is inexpensive, requiring very little equipment or special clothing.

3. It is always available. It can be accomplished on the street, track, path, road, or even in the basement.

4. It can be as competitive or noncompetitive as one chooses to make it.

5. Progress or gain is easy to monitor.

6. It is relatively safe with little risk of injury.

7. It is a lifetime sport.

8. It can be done alone, in pairs, or groups.

9. It requires no special skill or training and only a minimum amount of direction.

10. It consumes large amounts of calories and can be valuable in weight control.

*The daily run is more therapeutic than lying on the analyst's couch. Perhaps that's one of the problems with analysis— that it is not done every day and it must involve some other person on a rigid time schedule. Running makes us skeptical of rigid forms, patterns, and techniques.**

PHYSIOLOGICAL PROCESS

Running involves the use of the largest muscles in the body and therefore requires a great deal of energy. The energy required in distance running is so great that it can only be supplied by an *aerobic* source—oxygen, plus sugar or fat. Unlike short bursts of exercise, which can be accomplished with anaerobic energy (energy without oxygen), distance running consumes large quantities of oxygen and therefore drives the heart and lungs to work their hardest. It is this cardiopulmonary effect that is so important in maintaining general health and in preventing deterioration of the heart and other organs (Lorin, 1978).

Muscle contraction depends upon chemical reactions that provide the energy for movement. These reactions are the burning of fuel, such as sugar or fat. There are two types of energy-releasing chemical reactions that occur within the muscles. One reaction is the burning of sugar or fat by combining it with oxygen, called aerobic metabolism. Work supported by this type of chemistry is known as *aerobic work*. The total amount of energy that can be produced by aerobic metabolism is quite great, although the speed with which this energy can be released is somewhat limited. In general the amount of aerobic work that can be performed relates to those qualities that we call endurance and

*Reprinted by permission of the author from *Run to Reality* by R. Eischens, J. Greist, and T. McInvaille.

stamina. Only a relatively small amount of fuel is stored in the muscle itself. Most of it comes from other tissues, such as the liver, which provides glucose (sugar), and adipose tissue, which provides fatty acids (fats). These fuels must be transported to the muscles by the blood. Therefore the determining factors for aerobic work are not only the size and strength of the muscles, but also the richness of the blood supply to the muscle and the efficiency of the heart and lungs in delivering the necessary oxygen and fuel.

The other type of energy-producing chemical reaction is called *anaerobic* metabolism and refers to the chemical burning of fuel in the absence of oxygen. This reaction utilizes a special fuel, glycogen, a complex sugar compound that is stored in the muscle fiber. The energy from this anaerobic process is released very quickly. Anaerobic energy does not depend upon the availability of oxygen, but it does depend upon the amount of glycogen stored in the muscle. The total amount of anaerobic energy is, therefore, relatively limited. Anaerobic energy is available almost instantaneously, but is short-lived.

Anaerobic metabolism is most useful for sudden bursts of work or brief feats of strength, while aerobic metabolism is more appropriate for sustained muscle activity. As you might imagine, in most situations a combination of these two types of energy reaction occurs. However, if a muscle is made to work continuously and very heavily for a sufficiently long period of time, its glycogen stores will be depleted and it will be forced to work on a purely aerobic basis. This is the basis of aerobic training, in which the heart and lungs are maximally stressed by the need to deliver a great deal of oxygen to the muscles (Lorin, 1978).

According to Dr. Kenneth Cooper, author of *Aerobics* (1968), the effects of aerobic training include:

- lungs taking in and distributing oxygen more efficiently

- bigger and more blood vessels capable of carrying larger amounts of blood

- increased volume of blood with a greater total oxygen-carrying capacity

- healthier body tissue as a result of oxygen abundance

- strong and healthy heart that is "slow at rest" yet capable of accelerating to much higher work loads without undue fatigue or strain

- smoother digestion of food and elimination of wastes

- mental benefits including reduction in anxiety and irritability

- improved ability to relax and sleep.

GETTING STARTED

Most athletes train their minds by training their bodies. For many runners training the mind seems impractical; runners may go through their entire careers with the same essential weaknesses, such as inability to handle pressure or loss of motivation in the final part of a race. These problems continue as most athletes tend to train hardest at what they already do best, and assume that the training will somehow be magically comprehensive. There are few runners whose training fully develops areas in which they are weak.

According to Olympian Don Kardong, "records, personal or otherwise, are broken because people believe it is possible. They transcend other people's believed limitations"—as well as their own.

When planning a centered running program, first evaluate your running. Determine the areas that are your strong points and areas in which you are currently weak. Analyze various aspects of your running. Do you feel inferior when running with others? Do you have a finishing kick? Are you running in a coordinated and centered fashion? Begin to evaluate your best and worst runs. Keep a running log and record the characteristics of each run including your attitudes from start to finish. Look for patterns by repeating the process on a daily basis.

Once you have determined your strengths and weaknesses, examine your present training program to determine areas where strengths may be overdeveloped and weaknesses neglected. Don Kardong again, "The mental has been underplayed. Why? Largely because it is more difficult to define and analyze, and begs for individual differences even more than the physical arena. But it is certainly more interesting." Work on exchanging your old habits for some newer, healthier ones. You can create the quality of your run.

It is important to use variety in training to avoid boredom and improve running. Dr. Laurence Morehouse and Leonard Gross state the importance of variety in their best-selling book *Total Fitness:*

> *The jogger, for example, can run a mile in eight minutes every day for a year. At the end of the year, he will be in worse shape than he was at the end of the second month. For the first two months, running a mile would improve his condition. But if he continues to run the mile in exactly the same way, he will adapt to that demand, his response will diminish and he will begin to "decondition."**

CENTERED RUNNING STYLE

The essential principle of centered running is finding the style that wastes the least amount of energy. Jim Lilliefors (1978) believes that this relaxed approach to running can be enhanced by adhering to the following ideas.

1. Run erect. Ideally, the runner's upper body should be perpendicular to the running surface. The most common error is running with the pelvis and torso tilted forward; this puts undue strain on the legs and can cause general fatigue as well as hamper efficient breathing. Raising your chest and keeping it raised will help. Your head should be resting comfortably

*From *Total Fitness in 30 Minutes a Week* by L. E. Morehouse and L. Gross (New York: Simon & Schuster, 1973) by permission of Simon & Schuster.

on your shoulders rather than craning forward. Your back should be straight, not arched, and your buttocks tucked under.

2. *Avoid overlong or too-short stride.* Overstriding is one of the most common energy wasters. Similarly, a short, choppy stride simply tires the runner too soon.

3. *Land on the heels.* Some runners naturally land on the balls of their feet; they walk and run this way and always have. Others naturally land on their heels. The latter style is advantageous when running distances longer than a half mile. Landing anywhere but on the rear of the foot causes unnecessary leg strain and may lead to shinsplints. Optimally, the runner should land on the outer edge of the foot, toward the back.

4. *Develop an economical rhythm of footfall.* Your feet strike the ground approximately 1,600 times per mile. The lightest, quietest footfall is the most economical. When the foot lands it should have already passed the farthest point of advance and be on the backswing. It should land directly below the knee, squarely beneath the runner's body. Toes should be pointed straight ahead.

5. *Don't tense shoulders.* There is a common tendency to raise or hunch the shoulders while running. This is an unnecessary action that tenses the entire running style. Shoulders also shouldn't roll uncontrollably; they should remain loose, but stable.

6. *Carry arms low and relaxed.* Two frequent mistakes in running style are carrying the arms too high and running with arms stiff and elbows "locked." Carrying the arms too high leads to a shortened stride and undue tension in the shoulders. The locked elbow produces muscle tension in the upper body. Arms should be loose, one arm swinging smoothly forward while the opposite leg advances. If your arms are tense, use a sprinter's trick. Press your thumbs against your middle fingers. All the tension will flow to that point. Now release, and relax.

7. *Keep the face relaxed.* Oddly, the head and facial muscles have a tremendous effect on the relaxation of the rest of the body. The most commonly overtensed facial muscles are those at the base of the neck; the jaw muscles, just below and in front of the ears; the muscles around the eyes; and the ones that wrinkle the forehead. Relaxing these areas will bring about relaxation all over.

CENTERED BREATHING STYLES

Probably more than any other factor proper breathing is crucial to success in athletics and especially running. Oxygen serves as the body's major source of fuel. Our oxygen requirements increase markedly during running, which means that every cell needs extra nutrients, more energy, and metabolic exchange. An inadequate supply of oxygen from improper breathing can seriously interfere with strength, endurance, flexibility, concentration, and enjoyment. The following centered breathing styles will be helpful in running.

BELLY OR TOTAL BREATHING   Concentrate on using your diaphragm and stomach, not your chest, to expand and contract your lungs. Your chest and upper rib cage are extremely inefficient instruments for good sustained breathing.

TIDAL OR RHYTHMIC BREATHING   This uses a rhythm in which inhalations and exhalations correspond to ocean waves. The motion involves alternating acceleration and rest.

NOSE INHALE AND MOUTH EXHALE   For added energy and acceleration on hills or other challenges, inhale twice through your nose and exhale through your mouth twice. The two-part breathing will quickly remove the increasing buildup of carbon dioxide as well as return the body to proper breathing. Excellent strategy for combating fatigue. Experiment with different breathing tempos.

MEDITATIVE BREATHING   With this type of breathing the actual inhalation and exhalation matter less than concentrating on that breathing. The breath count is a common exercise here. For the entire duration of your run, count each breath that you exhale, up to ten. Once you reach ten, begin again. If your mind wanders and you lose count, start over. This will strengthen and will also make it easier to relax.

ALTERNATE MOUTH AND NOSE BREATHING Many runners practice naturally inhaling from the nose and exhaling from the mouth, and vice versa. This is mostly valuable as a rhythmic breathing exercise and as a means of demonstrating self-control.

SITKARI Clench your teeth and inhale air through your mouth with a snakelike sound. Exhale through the nostrils.

YOGA CLEANSING BREATH Inhale deeply through the nose, then quickly pull in your stomach so that the air is forced back out through the nostrils. This should be done 5 to 10 times at first and then eventually 20 times at once. Initially it might create a light-headed sensation. Stop when this occurs. It will disappear with practice.

WARM-UP BREATHING The following techniques for warm-up breathing are advocated by Philip Smith in *Total Breathing* for use in preparing for the run. The focus is to gear up the respiratory system, eliminate as much carbon dioxide as possible, and loosen up muscles.

1. *Handclasp.* This exercise primes the body with extra oxygen while at the same time loosening up the spine and upper torso. Standing, interlock the fingers of both hands, raise your arms above the head, and turn them inside out (palms out). Inhale using the belly breath. Then, lift the hands and stretch the body upward as far as they will go and inhale a second time to fill the top of the lungs. Now, bend sideways to the right as far as you can and let the breath out in a long, slow rhythm. Repeat, going to the left side. Repeat this ten times for each side.

2. *Bending Breath.* Inhale, using the belly breath. Do a toe touch

while breathing out with a single quick breath. As you come back up breathe in, using a long, slow rhythm. Repeat 15 times.

3. *Dangle Breath.* This process loosens the spine, especially the lower back. It also provides a fresh supply of blood and oxygen to the brain, getting rid of any feelings of fatigue or cloudy thinking. Inhale, using the belly breath. From the waist upward, let the body fall toward the floor and just dangle. As the body drops downward, expel all the breath in one large exhalation. Hang for ten counts and breathe deeply in as you rise. Repeat 10 times.

4. *Hissing Breath.* This process clears out any remnants of stale air in the lungs. It decreases the possibility of becoming short of breath or incurring fatigue. By cleaning out the lungs you are also making room for greater quantities of oxygen, which promotes greater stamina and better performance during the run. Inhale, using the belly breath. Tilt your head back so that your chin is pointing up in the air. Open your lips and force exhalation out between closed teeth, making a hissing sound. Bring the head back down and inhale. Repeat the process ten times.

Concentrate entirely on your breathing, as if you had nothing else to do. Through this breathing, you will not only discover the source of all spiritual strength, but also cause this source to flow more abundantly, and to pour more easily through your limbs. *

CENTERED RELAXATION

The optimal anxiety level has been described as a state of relaxed alertness. Too little or too much anxiety decreases performance and enjoyment. The centered athlete is balanced and

*From *Zen in the Art of Archery* by Eugen Herrigel. Copyright 1953 by Pantheon Books, Inc. Reprinted by permission of Pantheon Books, a Division of Random House, Inc.

aware of tension level and makes changes as they are needed.

The centering process of focusing creates a form of dynamic relaxation. The ability to focus is an important ingredient in athletic success. Peak performance occurs when a shift in focus from your performance to your purpose and plane occurs. The focusing process involves developing the ability to make fine tuning in performance to remove any unproductive activity.

You learn dynamic relaxation in the Jacobsen (progressive) method. While you are in motion, keeping a steady pace, slowly count to ten as you increase tension. Gradually tense your body all over, constricting the muscles, clenching the hands and feet, gritting the teeth. When you feel you're as tight as you can possibly be and still be able to move, you should be at the count of ten. Then, counting backward to one, slowly let loose your muscles, hands, and feet, and let yourself go slack. Let your body go limp. From this lowest tension point, increase your tension a notch or two, until you feel just right (p. 42).

At the finish of this exercise you'll be at an optimal level for performance, not so loose that you can't function, but not so tight that movement is restricted.

The advanced form of this process is called the *dynamic relaxation run*. This involves following dynamic relaxation with the same process applied only to the lower legs, ankles, and feet. As you run increase the tension, then let it fade gradually until you find a looseness or flipping action in your ankles that, if any more pronounced, would interfere with your running style. Keep searching back and forth, alternating tensing with relaxing, until you feel that you've got the ideal degree. Then move up to the knees, thighs, and hips, and repeat the process. Try to keep your lower leg area relaxed as you increase the tension in your thighs and buttocks, making yourself feel that you're running stiffly. Then gradually release the tension until you feel that you are slowing down, even wobbling. At that point, bring the tension back to the point at which you control the running stride once more. While practicing this procedure also try releasing the tension in your lower back to allow more than usual hip rotation. Such hip rotation should enable you to increase your stride length without altering your stride frequency (pp. 44–45). This little change could bring about a remarkable change in speed.

CENTERING FOR SPEED

The centered athlete knows the importance of participating with awareness and relaxation. To move faster, concentrate not on applying more power but rather on increasing relaxation. When an athlete moves a muscle to create a movement, two separate processes must occur. First, the muscle contracts to produce the movement, and second, it relaxes to return to its original position. Most athletic training concentrates on strengthening the contracting phase. The centered athlete also focuses on the relaxing component. Athletic performance and enjoyment result not so much from the swiftness with which you can contract your muscles but from the swiftness with which you can relax them so they don't act as brakes on your performance.

*Feel the flow
of the dance
and know
you are not running
for some future reward—
for the real reward is now!**

FIFTEEN EXPERIMENTS IN
CENTERED RUNNING

Running to Feel

Today as you run notice the internal sensations of your body and mind. Running allows you to expand your ability to experience yourself. While some people run to escape themselves, to get away from their feelings, you can run to experience yourself at deeper and deeper levels. With this attitude you come more into awareness of yourself with each step.

All experiences are to be felt. Even pain is a message to be listened to very closely. Rather than resisting it, experiment with

*From *The Zen of Running* by Fred Rohe. Copyright © 1974 by Fred Rohe. Reprinted by permission of Random House, Inc. and The Bookworks.

opening up to it with understanding. Allow it to speak to you. Is it telling you that you are trying too hard? Is it suggesting that you are running off-center to the front or to one side? Questions like these indicate that you are interested in learning about yourself and all your feelings. And with this kind of open attitude the moment-by-moment experience of running becomes charged with aliveness.

Other feelings come up as you run. You may feel fear, joy, anger, sadness, excitement. As running deepens deeper feelings emerge. The body is clearing out old stored-up feelings from the past. We do not have to take these feelings seriously, acting on them or turning them into a drama. All we need to do is feel them and run right through them. When you find yourself shutting down to your feelings you might experiment with breathing more deeply, opening up to them, allowing yourself to experience them. Many people are pleasantly surprised to find that when they open up to feelings, instead of resisting them, the feelings dissolve.

To establish the open attitude you may say to yourself: "I am willing to feel whatever I need to feel to bring me a greater sense of aliveness and harmony."

Running allows you to experience life more deeply. Part of life is negative, part is positive. By being willing to experience it all you run from a place of spacious openness.

The Looking Glass Run

Part of our human tendency is that we put ourselves subconsciously into growth experiences, because we secretly love to grow and feel more alive. But then we resist the lessons that those experiences are trying to provide. Let us see then if we can open up to the lessons of running and life as they flow toward us.

The way you run is the way you live. You are running to learn more about life. Running with a willing attitude to learn what you need to learn is an excellent way to grow in centering.

What does the way I am running symbolize about my life? Is it effortful? Does it lack joy? Is it boring? Am I running to escape something? Questions like these are not to make you feel bad, but to allow maximum learning to occur. If you find yourself feeling bad about asking these kinds of questions, then you can ask yourself why you think you have to feel bad about knowing more about yourself.

How about posture? What does the way I am holding my body tell me about the way I am holding my life? A common problem among runners, for example, is the tendency to get the top of the body out front, a posture of straining to get to the goal. This takes us out of harmony with ourselves and makes the run effortful.

By using the run as a mirror for life itself an infinity of rich learning can come our way.

What to Do When You're Not Feeling Centered

Being centered all the time is not a useful goal. Humans are not designed to be any one way all the time. Further, if you pursue a goal like being centered, the very effort of pursuit causes it to elude you. We will always be in the process of feeling centered, then losing the feeling, then getting it again. So the truth in life is not maintaining the feeling of centeredness, it is knowing what to do when you're not feeling centered.

Suppose you are out on a run and you don't feel very well. Your breath is labored, dull pain is everywhere, you have that tired feeling all over. How do you get from there to feeling centered? Certainly not by trying to feel centered, or making a vow, or criticizing yourself.

When in the grip of negative feelings, centering comes through allowing yourself to explore these feelings. Instead of trying to get away from the pain or the tiredness, then, you can open up to the feelings with an attitude of wanting to learn about them. At the moment you open to them, at the very moment you become willing to see them or feel them, centering takes place. There is no particular way you have to feel in life. Life is all about cycles of feeling. The secret is how you feel about how you feel. At the moment you feel all right about feeling bad, you feel all right.

Overcoming Inertia

For most of us running involves a struggle. For many the struggle is whether or not to get out of the chair. For others the struggle is whether or not to go the second block or the second mile, whether to finish the marathon or whether to stop at mile 22. We talked once with that excellent runner, Frank Shorter, just after he had lost a race by one second. For him a whole lifetime of running had come down to that final sprint, several seconds at the end of thousands of hours on foot. And the issue had been the same: the struggle.

To end that struggle once and for all let us simply be willing to listen to the wisdom of our bodies. Let us ask our bodies questions like: Does this tiredness I'm feeling today mean that I need rest or exercise? Body, do you want to go more slowly? Do you need to rest awhile before continuing?

We need to understand inertia, not overcome it. Let us ask ourselves why we are sitting in the chair. The questions are embarrassingly frank. Am I trying to die? Is my life not worth continuing? Am I afraid to experience life more deeply?

Being willing to ask questions like these is the answer. There are no right answers to how you should exercise, or how much. All you can do is deepen your relationship with yourself by expressing a willingness to find out more. And many have found an awesome secret. At the bottom of themselves, beneath the inertia, is a wellspring of boundless energy and positivity to draw on whenever you need it.

Inertia, then, no matter at what level you experience it, is something to be inquired into, seen through. In the willingness to look at it lies the answer, for that moment, of what to do about it.

Running as the Spirit Moves You

There is a part of us deep inside that seems perfectly willing to tell us, if we will listen to it, when it's time to go fast or slow. When you can become sensitive to the ebb and flow of inner energy, running with it instead of against it, the run can become a tireless, harmonious experience.

Here is one person's experience of how this inner energy feels:

I am flying like the wind down a long hill when somewhere deep inside I hear a calling to slow down. I respond, and I find myself riding the crest of my breath. A wave of ecstasy sweeps over me. I see that if I had continued to run fast I would have exhausted myself, pulling every ounce of energy out of my muscles. Sometimes that would be okay, but not today.

Now, on the flat again, I feel like slowing even more. A crawl, a shuffle, I'm almost embarrassed by how slowly I'm going. Now a gust sweeps through me and I fly again, catching the crest of energy as it surges through me. Higher, higher, higher—now slowing again.

So it goes. There is no right pace, no right way to do life. The rule for running is the same as for living: There are no rules. It is simply a question of learning to listen to ourselves, turning in to the center, going our own pace.

But won't that take forever? Won't we make mistakes? Of course. Who said we have to do it right?

Running to Breathe

Today, as you run, pay attention to the sound of the breath as it rushes in and out of your body. The quality of the breath, the way you breathe, can be a metaphor for the quality of life.

Notice whether the inhalation goes all the way to the limit of the breath. Notice the exhalation. Is it complete and full? The inbreath can be a metaphor for how deeply you are willing to experience life. The outbreath can be a metaphor for how deeply you are willing to express yourself in the world.

Is the breath tentative, ragged? Does it deeply nourish you? These are not questions meant to criticize, but to learn. Is it stingy, generous? Loving, fearful? All these are things to be seen, things to know about ourselves.

Most people breathe in order to run. Today run to breathe. Experiment with running to play with your breath. See how you need to run to breathe deeply and fully. See how slowly you must run to keep your breath from becoming painful or effortful.

Listen to the breath.

Running within the Breath

Today, as you run, experiment with staying just inside your breath. Even if it means a slow lope, even a walk, keep your movement just fast enough to expand the breath while staying within it. It's a delicate idea, hard to imagine, but if you run a hundred yards you will see what it means.

On the run we want to expand slowly, dancing along on the edge of the breath, letting it gradually expand to support our greater capacity for living. No effort.

So many runners push it too far and too fast, too soon. They forget that running is a dance, that it works best when it is no work at all. They run outside their breath, then collapse and wonder why they do not feel like running again.

Now you see what the secret is: staying just within the breath. When you do this, the breath naturally expands, allowing you each day to go farther and faster. It is exquisite, the way it works.

Running for Variety, Running for Stillness

There are times when it feels good to run in a routine, round and round, no ups and downs. Other times it's good to run for variety. Both paths have their rewards.

Routine has the advantage for using running as a meditation. Running around a track, for example, can free your mind so that it can float and transcend, or turn its attention to inner work.

For variety you can change your pace frequently or take on a new territory. Quick changes in pace, for example, can bring delight to a run that's gone flat or stale. Fresh terrain can bring both mystery and adventure to the run.

Today notice whether you feel like running as a meditation or as an adventure, or both.

Sneaking Up on the Dragon

In the old days knights rode out in search of dragons to slay. Now we know that the dragons are all inside of us, and that they are to be befriended and put to work instead of slain.

One dragon is the unpleasant part of our inner experience:

our pain, our negative thoughts and feelings. Another dragon is the awesome power that lies within, the limitless inner energy that we keep in check with fear. Running is an ideal way to learn to deal with these dragons. On a run, as we breathe more deeply and take on a deeper relationship with life, the dragons come to the surface.

We cannot chase dragons, we simply have to be willing to deal with them when they come. Then when it is time they will stride forward, one by one, to be embraced, befriended, danced with, loved, and welcomed into ourselves.

Then comes the power. By being willing and open to experiencing ourselves, all of ourselves, we get the payoff of a reservoir of energy that we can draw on infinitely. By befriending the dragon and accepting its fury we get to put its power to our own use.

You might say: "Today as I run I open myself to experiencing all of myself. I open myself to a deeper relationship with my inner energy."

Running for Space

Many people want a long life; fewer have considered the goal of a wide life. A wide life is open to the moment, experiencing everything as intensely as possible. A long life involves time, a wide life, space.

On the run we can open ourselves to occupying more space. We can open up space for experiencing all of our feelings: fear, sadness, compassion, love. We can open up to pain, ecstasy, forgiveness, passion. Nothing is too big to be experienced in space.

Space holds everything. Space contains all feelings, thoughts, all matter, all energy.

A thought for the run: "Today I am willing to experience space. I am open to being the source for all that exists."

Running for Answers

Running has the power of turning on the creative part of the mind. By allowing the body to experience the joy of movement the runner leaves behind for a while the noise on the surface of the mind.

Running can be a powerful problem-solving tool. The joy of movement takes us beneath the noisy surface of the mind to a deeper creative part. You have an opportunity, then, to use running as a way of finding answers to questions and problems on which the conscious mind is stuck.

The experiment is this: Take a question or problem, phrase it in the mind, indicate that you would like an answer, then take off on your run. You may be stuck for a solution to a problem at work, for example. You might phrase the problem by saying, "I do not know what to do about my relationship with my boss." You then indicate your willingness to solve the problem by saying in your mind something like, "I'm willing to solve this problem." Now, forget it all and go for a run. During the run you may find, as many have, that something happens deep in the mind, bringing up solutions that the conscious mind might never have thought of.

Running through Cycles

As you run you experience cycle after cycle of up and down, high and low. For every hill there is a valley. Even a high plateau sometimes seems like just another flat place.

What to do about these cycles, both those on the run and those on the path of life? To be aware of and experience them is really all you need to do. We create problems for ourselves when we fail to see that cycles permeate life. Then we resist both the up-cycle and the down-cycle. Resisting slows down the process, making the lows longer and lower and the highs more elusive. In other words if you find yourself heading down it is futile to effortfully pull yourself up. Best to look at the cycle, see what it's about, open up to it, feel it, taste it, then let it come back up naturally after you have gleaned the wisdom of the cycle.

Today as you run you might think: "I'm big enough to experience all cycles. Everything can occur within me. I am one with all the experiences in the universe."

Running for the Joy of Movement

Satchel Paige, one of baseball's greatest pitchers, once gave, as one of his rules for living, the following advice: "jangle gently as you move, so as to keep the vital juices flowing." We could use the same advice for running, because one of the benefits of running is the moment-by-moment joy of movement, the pure ecstasy of being in a moving human body.

Joyful running is not a place to get to, it is a way of getting places. It helps to open yourself up to experiencing, in each moment, as much as you can of the pure joy life has to offer. As you run you are building up mile after mile of new blood vessels in your body. This means that you are literally increasing your ability to enjoy life.

As important as the mind is to our lives, it must share equally with the life of the body. The body is a giant sensing machine, a tool of enjoyment.

Experiment today with allowing yourself to experience and express the pure joy of movement as you run.

Running for Unity

You can feel a sense of unity in yourself, a feeling of wholeness in which mind, body, and spirit are one. But on the run toward unity you first experience the barriers that stand in the way of a sense of unity.

If anger is the thing that keeps you from feeling whole, it will emerge as you run. If your block to wholeness is your mind (your beliefs, biases, opinions), then these will probably manifest during your run.

Wholeness cannot be actively pursued. It comes upon you as a surprise, a gift for being willing to look at and experience all of the barriers. This is not to say it takes a long time to experience unity. Your willingness to experience yourself can have results instantly.

Often, though, time and practice are involved, because each time you run you bring up the next set of things that need to be looked at and embraced in yourself.

It can help to establish your willingness to experience unity through your running. You can do this by allowing your mind to think something like: "As I run, I give myself total permission to feel unity with myself, others, and the world around me."

Running Free of Your Beliefs

As you run you go through layer after layer of beliefs about yourself and the world. Running can be a perfect way of freeing yourself from these beliefs.

Beliefs are often very limiting. You may have a belief that says, "Running has to hurt to be doing me any good." It is easy to see where our limiting beliefs come from. They are usually based on what people have told us or shown us, or on some experience we have had.

You can begin to dissolve your limiting beliefs by letting your mind know that you are willing to give them up. You might say, "I'm now willing to let go of any beliefs that are keeping me from my perfect experience of running." Or, if you want to use running as a way of clearing out any other limiting beliefs about life itself, you might say, "I'm willing to let go, as I run, of any beliefs that are keeping me from being all I can be."

MENTAL EXERCISES TO DO
WHILE RUNNING

Slow Running

"Pleasure varies inversely with speediness." Whenever you feel like it, center into a slow motion. Let yourself slow down as far as it takes. Take your thoughts and actions one at a time. Focus your attention on just how you run. Become aware of each muscular and body movement.

This activity can be enhanced by fantasizing that you are running in a room filled with liquids such as oil, honey, Jell-O, or helium.

Who Am I?

While running at a comfortable pace ask yourself the question "Who am I?" dozens of times. The first few answers will reveal your typical thoughts and feelings, but continued probing will yield different answers. Qualities that you only dimly perceived rise to complete awareness as your self-concept grows.

Coloring Your Run

While running in a centered fashion hold in your mind's eye your choice of a static uniform color that occupies your entire mental-visual field. Some colors, such as purple, red, yellow, and orange, develop feelings of warmth. Others, such as blue and green, are likely to cool the forehead.

Counting Steps

This is a simple exercise to keep the centered runner in the here and now. Simply count up to 25, 50, or 100. Count backward or by fives—as one method becomes habitual, do another. In activities like this it is not so important what you do as long as you can distract yourself.

Mantra Repetition

A *mantra* is a word or phrase repeated by the person meditating, vocally (chanting) or subvocally. As in many meditative exercises the goal is to repeat the mantra and do nothing else, training yourself to focus your awareness.

Mantras number in the thousands and exist in many languages. *Aum* or *Om* is an example of a mantra used in Indian religions.

Two schools of thought concern mantra selections. The first holds that the content, what the mantra means, is important, that the actual sounds themselves affect the body, personality, and essence of the meditator, waking him or her up to the higher self. On the other hand several Western scientists have done physiological research indicating that the repetition of any sound, even such words as *one* or *glub*, done in a meditative fashion, relaxes the body and alters consciousness as effectively as "mystical" sounds.

Some English mantras you might repeat as you run are:

- Preparation meets opportunity.
- The jewel in the lotus.
- We are one.
- White clouds, blue sky.
- See forever free.
- Be still and know.
- Trust your self.
- Flowing, growing.
- Peace begins within.
- You are what you think.
- Back to balance.

Fantasy Mind Pictures

While running in a slow, balanced fashion allow yourself to fantasize about winning the Boston Marathon, the Olympic Games, or another exciting event. Allow your body to change tempo and form with each aspect of the contest. Notice the thrill and elation of being a winner.

Other fantasy images you might try include:

- Think of soaring like a bird to new heights.
- Have the wind encapsulate you and pull you forward.
- Imagine a magnet pulling you toward a destination.
- Imagine a hand at the small of your back pushing you along.
- Look at distant runners and let their energy pull you along.
- Feel a skyhook holding you upright and pulling you over the ground.

Smiling

The centered athlete concentrates on smiling and enjoying all aspects of physical activity. This increases the fun and decreases the amount of energy expended as a smile uses only 14 muscles while a frown or grimace requires over 70.

One of the authors' friends, a runner and gifted poet who prefers to remain anonymous, offered us a poem about running that seemed to capture timelessly many of the ideas we have discussed.

RUNNING INTO THE ONE

I am running, running
running into the One.
I feel the wind in my face:
I am the wind.
A pain in my knee:
the pain is me.
A rusty bumper by the road;
I am the road and the bumper, too.
As I run I go through place after place
On my way to the One.
I pass through bliss,
fear,
sadness
pain
fantasies
memories
music
All flotsam of the mind,
All part of the One.
Then, without warning, it is upon me;
Ecstatic unity.
Oneness all around.
Everything is me,
I am you and he,
We are we.
Somewhere in the One I hear an owl shriek.
The One runs.

REFERENCES

COOPER, K. *Aerobics.* New York: Bantam Books, 1968.

EISCHENS, R., GREIST, J. AND McINVAILLE, T. *Run to reality.* Milwaukee: Madison Running Press/Bulfin, 1977.

FIXX, J. *The complete book of running.* New York: Random House, 1977.

HERRIGEL, E. *Zen in the art of archery.* New York: Pantheon, 1953.

LEONARD, G. *The silent pulse.* New York: E. P. Dutton, 1978.

LILLIEFORS, J. *The running mind.* Mountain View, CA: World Publications, 1978.

LORIN, M. I. *The parents book of physical fitness for children.* New York: Atheneum, 1978.

MOREHOUSE, L. E. AND GROSS, L. *Total fitness in 30 minutes a week.* New York: Simon & Schuster, 1975.

MOREHOUSE, L. E. AND GROSS, L. *Maximum performance.* New York: Simon & Schuster, 1977.

PORTER, D. *Inner running.* New York: Ace Books/Grosset & Dunlop, 1978.

ROHE, F. *The zen of running.* New York: Random House, 1974.

SMITH, P. *Total breathing.* New York: McGraw-Hill, 1980.

SPINO, M. *Running home: The body/mind fitness book.* Millbrae, CA: Celestial Arts, 1977.

SPINO, M. AND WARREN, J. E. *Mike Spino's mind/body running program.* New York: Bantam, 1979.

5

The shield:
a new approach
to centered tennis

by Scott Ford

Gay Hendricks writes about his encounter with Scott Ford, the author of the following article on The Shield:

Although I had heard of Scott Ford and his work by reputation, it was not until recently that I had the opportunity to experience the power of his radical new approach. Within ten minutes on the tennis court Scott had me playing better tennis than I had ever played in my life. The results have lasted, too. Tennis is much more fun for me, and I now easily beat players who before consistently beat me.

After my first session with Scott, I immediately encouraged him to write a book about the approach. I am happy to report that he is doing so; the following chapter is a taste of the essence of his technique.

Scott, winner of many championships in the West, is a teaching professional in Colorado.

One fine day a few years ago I got very lucky and found what it means to be centered on the tennis court. The experience came suddenly, although I had been a tennis player since I was twelve and a teaching professional all my adult life. Through a series of events I will briefly describe a door opened to me, and beyond that door was a pathway that led me on a journey to the center of my sport. It was not an easy journey, for it was also a journey into my own consciousness, my own essence. The path took me to a place I had known only in glimpses. It took me beyond tradition.

Recall a day when, for an unknown reason, everything seemed to come together for you on the tennis court. Your strokes were crisp, you met the ball squarely, you saw the ball more clearly than usual. As a result you may have stunned yourself, and your opponent as well. Back when I was playing in the juniors we called that experience "zoning," because when we were in that state of consciousness we always seemed to be in the right zone at the right time to make the right shot. We knew zoning had something to do with concentration, but we did not know how to get ourselves into that state. When it happened it just seemed to happen all by itself.

Ever since those days in the juniors I had been trying to pinpoint that elusive state of zoning. It was intangible, like a word on the tip of my tongue. Then one day I got lucky. While watching some of my students play in a mixed doubles tournament I noticed something to which I had paid little attention previously. What I was watching had nothing to do with the progress my students were making in the technical aspects of their game. Instead it had to do with the area in front of the player often termed the "hitting zone." I noticed that almost every time the ball got past the players' hitting zone they either made an awkward return or missed the shot altogether. Even the best technical player on the court had the same problem. Good technique didn't help much once the ball got past the hitting zone. Conversely, nearly every time the ball was struck within the hitting zone, regardless of the technique employed, the return was not only solid, but the ball was placed well, too.

This observation changed my way of playing and teaching. I had always mentioned the point of contact and the hitting zone in my lessons, but I saw I had not stressed it enough. So the next day I went out on the court with a friend of mine to see if I could find a different way of explaining this hitting zone. To do this I tried an experiment with my own game. I had been having trouble with my midcourt volley, so we started at the service line volleying the ball back and forth, and the first thing I noticed was that the ball was almost always getting past my own hitting zone. The reason was fairly obvious to me. I simply didn't know where my hitting zone was at all times. I knew it was somewhere out there in front of me, but there was nothing substantial, nothing tangible to tell me where it was at all times. So I did something very simple. I *pretended I had a large invisible shield, akin to a pane of Plexiglas, stretched across the width of the court at arm's length in front of me and extending as high as I could reach my racquet.* As odd as this idea seemed at first it made good sense because every ball now hit toward me would sooner or later touch a point somewhere along this imaginary shield, and if I made sure nothing got past this touchpoint on my shield, then, in reality, nothing would be getting past my hitting zone. I gave it a try, just to observe what would happen.

When we began, much to my surprise, not only did my volley instantly improve, but when the exchange ended I had to shake myself out of the concentrative daze I was in. To use the old saying: I was completely "zoned"!

"That's it!" I yelled, "That's what I've been looking for!" I started bouncing up and down, and I'm sure my friend thought I'd lost my marbles.

"What's with you?" he asked. So I showed him the idea of the shield, and sure enough, the same thing happened to him. He "zoned," and I watched as his game took a dramatic turn in effectiveness.

My friend happened to be a clinical psychologist whose doctoral dissertation had been on imagery, the process by which images are formed inside the mind.

"Do you know what you've done here?" he asked.

I wasn't sure what he meant, but deep in the back of my mind I knew I had stumbled onto something important.

"You have figured out a way to bring the Image State of Consciousness outside the mind's eye."

"Oh," I said. I knew very little about image states of consciousness apart from my lifelong experience as a daydreamer. I was more concerned with the fact that I had lucked onto something that seemed to work. Yet, somehow, my friend had stimulated an interest in me that I hadn't known existed. The door had been opened.

I began using the shield in my everyday lessons. It was easy to teach: Imagine an invisible shield spanning the court in front of you at approximately arm's length, extending as high as you can reach your racquet. Look for the point at which the ball will touch the shield and let nothing get past that point. Start up close with volleys and work your way back to the baseline. I was moved by the results. The only problem was that, even though the results with both beginners and advanced players were superb, the image state was so different, so radical, that even when it was working many of my students felt that it was simply too weird. I had run head-on into the stiffest competition of my life—doing something different in a world where tradition reigns supreme.

But it makes good sense, and is easily learned. Listen in on a typical lesson.

"Hi!"

"Hi!"

"This is going to be a little different, so keep an open mind, and act as an observer, just to see what it feels like when you try this."

"O.K."

"Start by standing midway into one of the service courts. Imagine what it would be like if you actually had a large pane of Plexiglas at arm's length in front of your face, spanning the width of the service court, and extending as high as you can reach your racquet. Get the picture?"

"Yup. A large pane of Plexiglas right out here in front of me."

"Now, what would happen if I hit a tennis ball at you?"

"It would bounce off the pane of Plexiglas."

"Right, and that pane of Plexiglas is standing right where you want to contact the ball. Any ball that I hit in your direction will eventually hit a point somewhere along this Plexiglas shield. The point where it hits your shield is also your point of contact. This shield forms a barrier across your hitting zone. But, unfortunately, Plexiglas is a bit too bulky to carry around on the court, so you'll have to go with your imagination."

"What do you mean?"

"Just pretend that you have an invisible shield right where your Plexiglas shield would be, and look for the exact point the ball will hit that shield."

"Wait a minute! Are you telling me to look at this shield instead of the ball?"

"Yes."

"How will I see where the ball is going?"

"While you are visualizing this shield, your eyes are still looking in the direction of the ball, they just aren't *focused* on the ball, they are focused on the hitting zone. Your eyes will still pick up the movement of the ball, but it will be a peripheral blur when it starts off. As it gets closer to your shield, however, it is also coming into your preset focus. It will get clearer as it gets closer."

"Oh."

"All you need to do is look for this touchpoint on your shield, and let nothing get past it."

"Sort of like defending my shield."

"Exactly. If nothing gets past your shield, then you can logically assume you have contacted the ball at your hitting zone."

"What about footwork?"

"Don't worry about your feet just yet. The only thing you need to think about is putting your racquet flat against this shield. If you can get your *hand* all the way out there, the rest of your body will follow, including your feet."

On my side was the most compelling feature of the shield: It worked. I knew it. I had watched it work a hundred times, and deep down inside I knew there had to be some logical reason behind it. So I sat down to figure it out logically. I wanted to get beyond mystical abstraction to find a traditional explanation of how and why it worked. My starting point was the logic of movement and countermovement: the movement of the ball as it flies across the net, and my corresponding countermovements to intercept it.

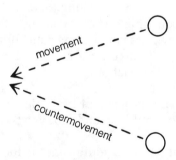

And because I was trying to relate the concentrative experience of "zoning" to this movement and countermovement diagram, I looked up the dictionary definition of concentration. I found the following definition: "the ability to bring together toward a common center: to focus."

It seemed to me that the most logical step to relate concentration to movement and countermovement was to find this common center, and immediately I saw that the common center of movement and countermovement was neither the ball nor the racquet, but the point where they came together—the point of contact. That fit in nicely with everything I had learned about concentration in tennis. The point of contact was definitely the one point on the court where my concentrative focus should be most acute.

So I added the point of contact of my diagram, threw in a few numbers to indicate the order in which things happened on the court, and finally marked in an imaginary shield stretched across the width of the hitting zone. (In reality the shield is only arm's length in front of you as you stand at point 2. For purposes of diagraming I have extended this distance.)

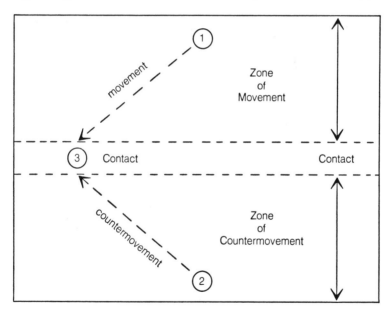

The first thing I noticed had nothing to do with concentration. Instead, I noticed that the court was now divided into three separate zones, the Zone of Movement, the Zone of Countermovement, and the Zone of Contact: the hitting zone. These three zones were all located within the boundaries of the court, giving me a diagram on which measurements in logic could be made. My measuring tool was one of the oldest and most logical systems of calculation known: triangulation, basic trigonometry.

My trigonometric skills were not world class, but I did notice, after studying this diagram, that it gave me a logical look at timing, one of the most difficult aspects of tennis to explain to a student.

An imaginary shield stretched across the zone of contact formed a reference point for calculating the relationship of movement and countermovement to time.

For instance: The movement of any ball hit in my direction will take a certain amount of time to get from my opponent's racquet to a touchpoint along this shield. Let's call that x amount of time. In terms of timing that gives me the corresponding x amount of time to get my countermovements from wherever I'm standing on the court to the same touchpoint on the shield. In mathematical terminology: x movement in time should equal x countermovement in time.

In other words, if my countermovements actually get to the touchpoint on the shield simultaneously with the movement of the ball, then in fact x countermovement *did* equal x movement in time, and that's good timing.

If nothing else I had chanced onto something that enabled me to define timing logically, in a way that made sense to my students. In terms of total countermovement two aspects were involved: the qualitative aspect, "how" you do your stroke, and the quantitative aspect, "how much" of that stroke you do. Most of the stress in teaching tennis is on the quality aspect of countermovement, "how" to do the stroke. But can the total countermovement be correct if quantitatively it takes too long and the racquet never reaches the proper depth of contact? Once movement gets past the zone of contact you are in trouble. Movement usually wins, and you get the feeling your swing was too late.

I found that a reverse approach to teaching countermovement was a nice solution. By making simultaneous contact with the touchpoint on the shield, the quality of the countermovement may not have looked perfect but quantitatively it was correct. The timing was right. Teaching the qualitative aspect of the stroke *after* my students learned the timing aspect, the quantitative aspect, proved a lot easier than the traditional method of teaching students the "how" of a stroke, then sending them out on the court into the real world of "how much."

Yet the simple act of visualizing this shield still seemed too strange for some of my students to attempt during a match situation. The fact that the shield worked for them in practice was often not a good enough reason to use it in a match! Under the stress of competition the shield often fell.

This line of reasoning baffled me at first, but practice and competition are polar opposites, particularly when the center of attention in competition is winning rather than competing. There's an old saying in tennis: Your opponent is the *ball*, not the player. But try telling that to a couple of housewives each of whom thinks the other is calling bad lines! Or to a championship-caliber kid whose victory-hungry father is watching from the sidelines.

The whole problem I was facing kept boiling down to the strange feeling of visualizing an imaginary shield: concentrating on the shield rather than concentrating on the ball. For years I had drilled my students to concentrate on watching the ball, then suddenly I was telling them *not* to concentrate on watching the ball, but to concentrate on an imaginary shield. Quite a few of them obviously felt I had spent too many hours standing in the hot sun, but the majority who were willing to give it a try found that it radically improved their games.

But there was still something missing. Concentrating on the shield still didn't explain why it seemed to bring a player's game together, or how it seemed to solidify the physical, visual, and mental skills involved in countermovement. So I went back to my diagram hoping to find an answer, and after some serious studying in my spare time, I finally put down all the facts as I understood them.

First, by visualizing the shield, a player is both mentally and visually focusing on the hitting zone. To visualize the shield at all, not only must you focus your eyes on it, you must also concentrate on it. Visually and mentally your focus is locked onto the hitting zone. Two of the three skills involved in the countermovement package (visual and mental) are already in the proper place. All that is left is to get the racquet to the touchpoint simultaneously with the ball.

Second, the lens of the human eye functions like the lens of a camera. Any object held outside the focal setting of a camera will gather in visual acuity as it is brought into the camera's focal setting. The same situation occurs when your visual focus is pre-established at the hitting zone. The ball may start out as a blur, and, indeed, it will, but as it gets closer to your preset depth of focus, it will gather in visual clarity. Which accounts for the reason I was seeing the ball so well at my point of contact. Instead of constantly switching my focus back and forth from a far field of focus to a near field of focus, I simply held my focus at the hitting zone and let the ball gather in clarity as it got closer.

The third fact helped to explain the odd sensation of the daydreaming that I would get while I was playing. Visualization, or the image state of consciousness, is a mode of consciousness associated with the right hemisphere of the brain.

Hemispheric brain research suggests that the left hemisphere acts in a dominant fashion, processing information in a very sequential, analytical way, while the right hemisphere processes that same information in a spatial, holistic way. In our normal state of consciousness the two hemispheres of the brain perform in this dominant-subdominant fashion. The left brain is essentially switched on, while the right brain is switched off. But when you visualize the shield the right hemisphere is switched on, and what you may have is whole-brain concentration.

Another interesting characteristic of the right brain is that it is also associated with eye-hand coordination. Spatial relationships and eye-hand coordination both play fairly important roles in tennis, and by visualizing the shield you can bring them both into full working potential. It *will*, though, feel different at first.

The fourth fact tied them all together. The radical difference in visual focus could be explained through the logic of the working eye in relation to focal depth. The seemingly automatic physical coordination and the strange sensation of this altered state of consciousness could be explained through the characteristic functionings of the right brain. But there was something mysterious still involved. What was my brain actually doing while I was concentrating on the shield? What was going on inside my mind while all this movement and countermovement was going on outside?

I knew, in rather unscientific terms, that the brain works as a receiver-processor-sender, like a computer. It was receiving the visual stimulus of the ball's movement through my eyes, processing that information, then sending out motor impulses to relate the countermovements of my body to the movement of the ball.

That wasn't what was happening, though. I was not looking at the ball. I was looking at the shield. My brain was receiving the visual stimulus of the ball's movement as it related to the *shield*, processing that information, then sending out motor impulses that coordinated my physical countermovements as *they* related to the shield.

There was a subtle difference there, but I didn't know what it meant. So I looked at my diagram once again, and suddenly it hit me. I had been looking at it all the time. It had been right in front of me, but I'd been looking for something complex.

It had to do with one of the first things I did on the diagram. When I had divided the court into three separate depths, the Zone of Movement, the Zone of Countermovement, and the Zone of Contact, I had also numbered the sequence of events as they actually occur on the court. Movement occurs first, then countermovement, then contact. One—two—three.

What this has to do with concentration and the way in which the brain relates visual stimulus to motor response may not be immediately apparent, until you realize that once your opponent hits the ball, her point of contact is finished. Movement has been set. It is a *past* occurrence. Your countermovements, since you are doing them, necessarily occur in the *present*. And, until the exact moment your racquet strikes the ball, the point of contact remains a *future* occurrence.

Movement—Countermovement—Contact. The past, the present, and the future as they relate to the sequence of hitting a tennis ball.

That was the subtle difference: the way in which my brain was relating these occurrences in time. And there was one more aspect. Where there is time there is also space. They are a continuum. One does not exist without the other. Just as yesterday had its own time, it also had its own space. Today, right now, the present, also has its own time and space. Tomorrow, the future, will also have its own time and its own space.

The same thing holds true with the sequence of events that

occurs on a tennis court. The past (movement) has its own space—the Zone of Movement. The present (countermovement) has its own space—the Zone of Countermovement. The future (contact) has its own space—the Zone of Contact.

The entire depth through which the ball moves, as it related to the total sequence involved, is a *past depth*.

The entire depth through which you make your counter-movements is the *present depth*.

The depth where you plan to contact the ball, the hitting zone, is a *future depth*.

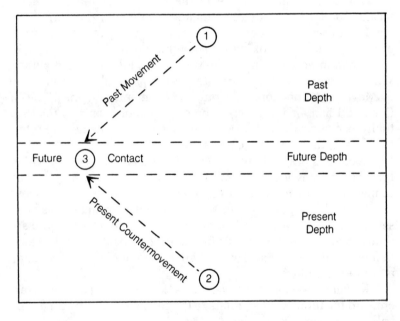

What I thought to be nothing but a simplified look at movement, countermovement, and contact was now something more—much more. I was looking at time and space on a tennis court. Logically, when I was concentrating on the shield, visualizing it, I was actually focused on the future as it relates to the sequence of movement, countermovement, and contact.

Through the simple act of imagining an invisible shield stretched across my hitting zone, my brain was receiving the visual stimulus of past movement as it related to future contact, then sending motor signals to my body that related my present countermovements to this same point of future contact. No wonder everything was coming together, my brain was relating the past and present to the future.

Perhaps that's what Webster meant when he said: "the ability to bring together toward a common center; to focus."

Yet there was still the indisputable strangeness of how it felt to focus on the shield. But is that strange feeling actually a flaw, or is it simply the way it feels when both hemispheres of the brain are working in unison? Only when both hemispheres of the brain are focused on the common center can concentration truly be called total. Whole-brain concentration. Concentration in its purest form. The essence. The Centered Athlete.

One thing is certain. The shield works for those who will take the step beyond tradition. The difficulty in that step lies in its simplicity. But which is easier? To remember something in your past: to recreate the steps you have already taken? Or to image the future: to step into the unknown, to see what you have only glimpsed before?

What lies beyond that door of tradition cannot be explained in words. In the end it is a feeling, a sensation of freedom, an awareness of mind and body. On the page they are abstractions, but they are real when felt in your body and mind. They are as real as the song of sport, the harmony between athletes and athletics. They are as real as the common center of tennis: the point of contact, the past and the present brought together in the future. As real as opening the door.

The centered racqueteer: lessons in centered tennis

with Terry Jones, M.D.

In this chapter we explore the idea of centering on the tennis court in more detail. Terry Jones, a psychiatrist and champion tennis player, has assisted many thousands of people to become more centered in their lives. The following lessons grew out of his conversations with the authors; they weave together life, psychology, and tennis into a whole.

The Basic Concept of Centering

Being centered has many different meanings on the tennis court. In singles the player must constantly return to the center of the court after each shot to be in the optimum position to receive the return. In doubles centering can mean the act of hitting the ball down the middle to take advantage of the lower net height and to increase the likelihood of the ball staying in bounds. Centering also can mean the physical position of the player's body at the time of stroking the ball. It means to have the feet firmly on the ground, knees bent, shoulders turned, and the racquet in full ready position.

Many experiments can facilitate centering on the court. Try this one. Go onto the court by yourself, with no ball, racquet, or opponent. Picture a ball being hit to you, and go through the motions of running to where the ball will appear, placing your feet, turning your shoulders, and putting your arms in the full ready position to swing through the ball. You can also conduct this experiment entirely in your mind, by picturing and feeling the various steps in the sequence. You can then extend it to the court in the heat of play.

Keeping Your Eye on the Ball

Keeping your eye on the ball is related in life to the central problem of staying in the present. Life is so much simpler when we are in the here and now, free of the weight of the past and the uncertainty of the future. Watching the ball continuously is absolutely crucial to the games of tennis and life. In any game you will go through thousands of alternations between having your eye on the ball and not having your eye on the ball. The ideal is to stay with the ball all the time, and until we reach this ideal state we must learn what to do when we find ourselves out of the present, our eyes elsewhere. In other words centering is the art of knowing what to do when you're not centered.

Try this experiment. As you begin play set your mind to work by saying something like this: "Today as I play I would like to keep my eye on the ball. I would like to notice where my mind goes when I slip out of watching the ball, and I would like then to return to keeping my eye on the ball." By setting your goal in this manner you not only remind yourself to keep your eye on the ball, but you also learn what kinds of things take you away from keeping your eye on the ball. Does dwelling on the last shot keep you from watching the present one? Are you too obsessed with winning to be enjoying the moment? Are you concerned about people watching you from the sidelines? We all have different mind ripples that take us from the here and now. See if you can find out what yours are.

Getting a Grip

In life, and in tennis, your grip will need to change with the circumstances. On ground strokes you will want to have a firm grip and a stiff wrist. On an overhead shot or a serve you may wish to loosen the grip to get more snap in the wrist. Beyond these considerations is whether or not the grip feels centered to you. Regardless of whether you are using the western or eastern grip, or the continental grip, the hand must feel centered on the racquet handle at the time of the stroke. Each grip, if centered correctly, will open up the face of the racquet for maximum impact at the moment of contact. One of the cardinal questions of life is whether we are willing to face life directly or whether we approach it obliquely, from an angle. You have an opportunity to study this issue as you grip the racquet and make contact with the ball. Before play you may set your mind in a fruitful direction by resolving: "Today I would like to meet the ball squarely, from a centered position. I would like to make maximum contact with the ball. I would like to learn the ideal grip for the situation, and I would like to see what I need to learn in order to have the perfect grip."

Timing

The timing involved in stroking the ball is an important concept for the player to consider. Hitting the ball too early may be a reflection of a general pattern in day-to-day living of being overly anxious and anticipating to an unnecessary degree. Hitting the ball too late could reflect another pattern, such as always waiting too long or delaying one's actions in life. The exact timing of impact with the ball is extremely important in terms of the follow-through. Hitting the ball too early or too late will result in an interruption of the flow of your stroke and make it more difficult to follow through completely so that you are adequately prepared for the next stroke.

Timing is affected by where the player wants to place the ball, the position of the opponent on the court at the time of the stroke, and how much pace the player wants to have on the ball at the time of the stroke. These nuances in timing are very similar to life situations that require consideration of a number of factors before taking action. If you simply try to hit every ball with the same timing, you will become very predictable and will not have the variety in your games that will keep your opponent off balance.

It is important to note here that it is quite common for older, more experienced players to have a greater variety of timing in their shots and to vary the pace of the ball as well as its placement, whereas younger players will frequently try to overhit the ball and be more powerful and, hence, make many more mistakes. Next time you play notice the variety of shots in your repertoire and the timing with which you deliver them. See if you are giving your opponent the gift of variety and challenge in your shots.

Keeping the Ball in Play

Keeping the ball in play is crucial. In relationships staying engaged and keeping the flow of communication going is the only way to resolve differences and problems. It maintains aliveness. In tennis the player who keeps the ball in play more will most likely come out the winner. Of course, in life, if both people in a relationship keep the flow of communication going, they both come out winners. The best way to keep the ball in play is not to overpower the ball but to make sure that one is centered at the time of each stroke. If you keep your eye on the ball at all times during play, and avoid the temptation to go for outright winners all the time, you will very likely find that you win more often.

Different Strokes: The Ground Stroke

The ground stroke is used with the player back toward the baseline. The feet are positioned so that for a right-handed player the left foot is out in front of the right with the legs comfortably spread, the knees bent to a considerable degree, and the shoulders turned so that they are almost perpendicular to the net. The grip for the forehand for a right-handed player is the eastern grip and the racquet position should be with the arm almost completely extended and pointed toward the backstop behind the player.

The backhanded ground stroke for a right-handed player uses a western grip and has the right foot even farther in front of the left and toward the sideline than was true for the forehand. That is, the shoulder turn is more exaggerated; you can even exaggerate the turning of the shoulders to the point that you are looking over your shoulder as you hit the ball. The backhand is actually a more natural stroke for a player because the shoulder of the arm that is hitting the ball is closer to the ball than it is with the forehand. Most players do not realize this and have a great deal of difficulty initially with the backhand. Once that stroke becomes more natural and centered the player often finds that the backhand is much stronger than the forehand.

Staying back at the baseline and using ground strokes is quite a valuable strategy. However, that strategy must be flexible because in the games of life and tennis it sometimes becomes necessary to be more aggressive and assertive. This can be accomplished by approaching the net and taking the initiative. What strategy is used, of course, will depend upon how the match is going, what the other player's weaknesses and strengths are, and what type of game the other player is using.

Different Strokes: The Volley

Coming to the net means you must learn how to use the volley. The volley is a stroke that usually occurs inside the service line and is characterized by the player facing the ball more squarely, in an open stance toward the net, than was true for the ground stroke. For the forehand volley a right-handed player uses the continental grip, and the left foot is out in front of the right, with not as much turning of the body or shoulders as was true for the ground stroke. Try to meet the ball well out in front of your body; you should be able to see the ball hit the racquet out in front rather than at your side or behind you when you are volleying. Use the continental grip with the backhand volley because this allows you to be more versatile at the net and have more time for the stroke if you are not changing the grip. The feet are slightly turned with the right foot in front of the left and the ball should be met in front of the player. Here it is very important that your grip be extremely firm, your wrist stiff, and your follow-through in the direction that you want the shot to go. The knees are bent less on the volley than on the ground stroke.

The volley is played closer to the net, sometimes within three or four strides of the net. It is a very important stroke in gaining an advantage in the game. Being closer to the net allows one to angle shots more for winners, allows one to hit the ball much sooner during play so that the other player has less time to react, and requires a great deal of finesse as well as strength. Many mistakes are made at the net and, hence, the player must capitalize on close-to-the-net plays. An analogy in life is that in a very close relationship one stands a chance of having a much greater impact on the other person than if one stays back and keeps distance, such as playing at the baseline. Without question a much more exciting game occurs when the player approaches the net, and the same is true in life. Being cautious is certainly part of relationships, too, especially in the early stages, but players should eventually develop other aspects of their game to move closer to the net or to the other person and achieve more excitement and variety.

Different Strokes: The Overhead

The overhead shot occurs when the other player has lobbed the ball high into the air. Here, being centered when hitting the ball is crucial. The common grip used for the overhead is the backhand grip or western grip. This is used because it opens up the face of the racquet for maximum force upon hitting the ball. However, one's grip can be adjusted with this shot, depending upon the placement that is desired. There is usually time with a lob to make a grip adjustment. The feet are slightly turned, though not as exaggeratedly as with the ground stroke. Keeping one's eye on the ball until it meets the racquet is extremely important. There is a tendency to drop one's head just before hitting an overhead, and this can result in a disaster. The analogy in life would be not paying attention to the last detail just before executing a particular action. The firmness of the grip in an overhead stroke can be varied and frequently is not as firm as with other strokes because of the need for the wrist snap. This gives the player much greater accuracy as well as power or spin on the ball if so desired. A powerful and accurate overhead stroke is a key element in a winning strategy in tennis because it is a stroke that can allow you to hit more winners than any other. When an overhead is being hit to you it means that your opponent is probably working very hard to find a way to get the ball past you and, as a result, has had to hit it high into the air in hopes that you will make a mistake. The player who has a strong overhead will not be vulnerable to this strategy.

Different Strokes: The Serve

The serve is a key stroke to the centered tennis player because you may use it to study how you initiate actions in your life. In much of tennis the lessons to be learned are how to react to different situations under stress. On the serve you may study how you act rather than react. The advantage is with you when you serve because of your ability to know ahead of time where you are going to place the ball and how hard you are going to hit it. Your opponent has to guess at both of these elements. Notice your feet as you serve. They should be turned somewhat sideways toward the net, the legs only slightly bent and the shoulders also turned considerably toward the net. Watching the ball on the serve and hitting it at its peak are crucial. The grip used is often the backhand grip because it allows for more spin on the ball and allows the server to come up over the top of the ball, even making the ball jump with the spin as it hits the opponent's playing surface. The spin makes it much more difficult for the opponent to hit the return shot.

The serve should be varied as much or more than any other stroke in tennis. Constantly hitting the serve to one place and with the same amount of pace allows the other player to become better able to return. A serve with a considerable amount of top spin tends to loop over the net and fall somewhat short. This serve forces the other player to move forward and throws off his timing. A hard, flat serve can be used as a way of forcing the other player to change timing and swing early because of the pace on the ball. Putting sidespin or the American twist on the ball not only causes the ball to jump as it comes off the opponent's surface but also will tend to move to one side or the other depending upon the twist. The twist forces the opponent to be off balance when returning the shot.

Notice your follow-through as you serve; your racquet should come up over the ball and completely down and through, letting the racquet come back toward the right leg for a right-handed player. This motion allows you to lean into the ball so that you can be on your way to the net following the serve. Coming to the net following a serve, if it is well paced and well placed, will give you a tremendous advantage. Once you are at the net the other player has less time to react to each shot and is forced to play a shot that you will likely have a good chance of putting away. The so-called serve and volley game, which is simply utilizing one's serve to advantage by coming into the net after each serve, can be extremely effective as witnessed by the world championship caliber of Martina Navratilova's game. Initially she was not able to master this style because she was overly anxious and aggressive. However, with practice she now has not only the strength of her serve but the touch and finesse of her volley. With this combination she has become a very strong player.

The Big Lesson

In the games of life and tennis correct form is important. How you meet the ball, and meet what comes your way in life, determine whether or not you are a winner. Keep in mind, though, that the winner is not always determined by the score. The winning player is one who is learning how to be more centered, who is learning how to live in the present, who is celebrating the joy of movement.

Tennis is a superb way to study your form in life. It is a game that will let you know quickly when your form has slipped. It will show you a hundred times a set how to lose form, then regain it and become centered again. By participating in tennis as a process of centering, you win big no matter the score.

7

Centering on the mountain: experiments in centered skiing

For pure exhilaration few things can match the sensations of skiing. There is the mountain itself, an intricate, powerful work of art that has its own personality, its own energy. There are the skiers, coming to the mountain with their own intricacies, energy, and personalities. Then there is the paraphernalia, boots, poles, and boards, often chosen with care and at outrageous expense, the meeting place between skiers and mountain.

The combination of these factors, plus the weather and a hundred other variables, brings to skiing a mystique that can make passionate the most modest of persons. Skiing is a mental sport, a matter of attitudes rather than muscle. There is no best body for skiing, no right type of person. We once followed a small, bespectacled, dumpy man down a Colorado mountain. He skied the trail like he was making love to it. This he did with incredible precision and nearly demented speed. Later we shared a chairlift with the man and were impressed to find that he was a banker playing hooky for the day.

As the poet Gerard Manley Hopkins said, "O the mind, mind has mountains; cliffs of fall/Frightful, sheer, no-man-fathomed." In skiing there is an exquisite relationship between mind, body, and mountain. Learning to ski the mountains of the mind has an immediate effect on your ability to maneuver the mountain beneath your skis. And the physical mountain can teach you much about life. The experiments that follow are designed to weave together mind, mountain, and life into a harmonious whole.

Preparing the Mind

Today, as you ski, open your mind to learning from the mountain everything you need to know about skiing and life itself. These

116

learnings can be as lighthearted or as serious as you need them to be. If you need to overcome fear of falling, for example, the mountain may give you the experiences of fear and falling. This it does to assist you. If you need to learn more about relaxing and enjoying life, the mountain has a thousand lessons on that subject, too.

So, you can go to the mountain as a student. With this attitude you open yourself to an immense array of experiences. You will undoubtedly learn things you never dreamed of learning. Others may go to the mountain with the intention of having dominion over it. The mountain has lessons for them, too.

Centered skiing does not mean you have to be continuously aware of all the lessons of life. That would be impossible, and no fun. What centered skiing is about is being *willing* to be aware. It is skiing with a willingness to learn whatever the mountain is trying to teach you.

Notice that the way you ski is the way you live. Notice what comes up inside you as you ski. Notice the posture you hold, your breath, the way you relate to others on the hill.

Note also that none of these suggestions needs to keep you from having fun. Skiing is more fun than practically anything, and these experiments can be carried out in a lighthearted manner that doubles the fun by adding the exhilaration of learning to it.

What You Resist Runs You

One of the facts of life is that what you resist in your mind begins to run your life. You can see this fact plainly on the mountain. If you resist, for instance, if it is not all right with you to fall, the fear of falling will run your life. You will either fall a lot, or you will ski so stiffly and defensively that you won't have any fun.

Two of the major things we tend to resist are our own feelings and the wisdom the outside world is trying to bring to us. Inner emotions, such as fear, excitement, and joy, are seeking to be experienced by us. The outside world has much to teach us as well. Let us see, then, as we ski, if we can drop our resistance. Can we let it be all right for us to experience all of ourselves as we ski? Can we open ourselves completely to information from the outside universe?

Skiing with no resistance in your mind means that you are

free to experience everything. What a magnificent attitude to bring to the mountain!

Skiing in the Present

As you ski you may notice that your mind slips in and out of the present. One moment you are keenly focused on what is actually happening—the sounds, feel, sights of skiing right then and there. A moment later your mind is elsewhere—back at breakfast, replaying a conversation, planning the evening. This is the way the mind works, back and forth, in and out.

You may notice that your best skiing is when you are *right there* in the present. Perhaps someday all your time on the mountain will be in the present. Until that is achieved what you can do is watch the comings and goings of your mind, noticing what takes you out of the present. For one person worry may take them away from the here and now, for another it may be music in the mind or chatter. For the author who was preparing this chapter on a skiing trip, mentally writing this chapter repeatedly took him out of the present when he was on the mountain.

Let us be careful here lest we think that being in the present is *good* and not being in the present is *bad*. This way of thinking would lead us to *try* to stay in the present, and of course the very act of trying would take us even further from the present.

You may say, "Today as I ski I am willing to watch my mind come and go from the here and now. I'm interested to see where it goes when it leaves the present and what it brings back."

Telling Mind Mountains from Real Mountains

As you have seen the mountains are in the mind. As you inquire into these mountains you will of course find them to be illusory. A mountain made of mind-stuff can be dissolved in a flash. Fear, for example, is a mind mountain that has no reality once you experience it. When you are unwilling to see and feel it, it can seem awesome. But the moment you open up to it it dissolves like fog in the presence of the sun.

As you see and dissolve the mind mountains you can begin to

appreciate the actual mountain beneath your skis. Once you are no longer filtering the mountain through your mind you can have an actual experience of the mountain you are on. The same is true of life. While we filter life through our beliefs and other mind-stuff, it is difficult to have an actual experience of it.

You and the Mountain Are One

While it may feel like you and the mountain are two separate entities, this is not really the case. We are trained at an early age to see the separateness in ourselves and the world. We think that our feelings are not part of us, or that our minds are separate from our bodies. We are also trained to see the differences between ourselves and other people. We hear that we should not feel one with people because of their color, sex, or class difference, for example. So, too, we are conditioned to feel separate from nature: The mountain and you are enemies, at odds. One must conquer the other.

In reality, though, it is all one universe, and we are all equals within the whole. Our troubles begin when we withdraw from that sense of unity and think of ourselves as separate. The mountain is a superb place to work out this issue of separateness versus unity, because the mountain and your body give you immediate feedback on whether you are feeling separate or unified.

When you are skiing from a place of separateness your body feels like it is efforting. Tension is there (often in the neck, shoulders, and legs) along with a vague feeling that this is not as much fun as it should be. A feeling of separateness from the mountain brings with it a wariness on your part that it is out to get you.

Relax, the mountain is your friend, is your brother, your sister, your teacher. You and the mountain are one, and you are separated only in the mind. When you let go of your feeling of separateness and relax into a feeling of unity with the mountain, a new relationship with it begins. Skiing then can become a dance, a partnership between equals.

You might initiate a thought that says, "Today I'd like to ski in such a way that I enhance my sense of unity with myself, others, and with nature."

Skiing Free of Your Personality

On the mountain you can either ski from inside your personality or you can ski to be free of your personality. In reality you will probably go back and forth between those two positions until you find a way of skiing that is uniquely you.

When you are skiing from inside your personality you will notice patterns repeating themselves. You may notice, for example, that you often fall when turning right, or that you tend to be critical of yourself in your mind. Body tension is another cue that your personality is getting in the way. Seeing that these things are true is the first step in getting free of them.

When you ski free of your personality you feel alive, exhilarated, close to yourself and the mountain. It is that feeling of freedom that comes not from irresponsibility but from seeing things the way they really are, being who you really are.

There Is No Limit to Feeling Good

Most of us have beliefs that keep us from feeling as good as we could. Such beliefs tell us that "there's something wrong with feeling good" or "if it feels good it must be sinful." Beliefs like these not only keep us from feeling good, they can make us feel bad.

As you ski you have the opportunity to expand your ability to feel. You stretch the upper limit to feeling good just by letting it be all right for you to feel as good as you can.

A good thought for the mountain is, "There is no limit to how good I can feel. I open myself to all the good feelings in the universe."

Skiing from the Center

Notice where your center is in your body as you ski. The actual physical center of your body is down around your navel. Often, though, because of tension and anticipation, we pull our center up into our chest, shoulders, neck, and head. Doing that takes us out of the true sense of centeredness that comes from being in touch with the center of gravity deep within the body.

Notice any straining of the neck or hunching of the shoulders.

120

Notice if you are straining with your eyes, or leaning forward over your skis. Skiing from the center means to relax the upper parts of the body, settling into a balanced position over your skis.

The feeling of skiing from the center is something that's relaxed into rather than pursued. It is already there; the perfect position is waiting for you to relax into it.

Skiing to See

As you ski you have the opportunity to see in more subtle ways than you may have in the past. There may be a moment, for instance, if you are open to it, when your vision shifts and you begin to perceive things in a new way. You may see the contours of a slope as lines of energy that flow in certain ways.

We get so locked into seeing the world in conditioned ways that we sometimes overlook aspects of the world that could assist us in moving through it.

As you ski there is no particular new way to see; the only thing to be done is to be willing to let go of the old, conditioned way. Listen to one skier's experience:

Strictly a novice, I had stuck to the wide, easy slopes every time I skied. I particularly avoided the mogul fields. The bumps terrified me. Then one day I paused at the top of a moderate mogul run to watch the "good" skiers go down. Suddenly I saw the way to do it. There seemed to be a streaming flow of energy down the run. Some skiers followed it, others seemed to buck it. Wow, I thought. I can do that! So I took off down it, and for the next 20 seconds I was one of the good skiers. I got so into following those streaming lines of energy that I forgot I wasn't a very good skier.

A thought for the day: As I ski I am open to new ways of seeing. I am willing to let go of my old way of seeing the world.

Skiing to Breathe

The breath is our intimate, moment-by-moment connection with life. It can also be a superbly sensitive diagnostic tool to let us know where our center is. Notice the quality and depth of your inhalation and exhalation. Does the inbreath fill you up completely? Does it deeply nourish you? And now the outbreath. Is it exhaled completely? Do you, in other words, fully express yourself? Questions like these may at first sound silly. Later, as you see the connection between your life, your breath, and the sport in which you're involved, questions like these may take on a deep meaning for you.

Notice the quality of your breathing as you ski. Let the skiing be a way to learn how to breathe. Your experience on the mountain will be directly related to the experience of your breath. There is no right way to breathe, but there is a way of feeling about your breath that can make a difference on the mountain. It is a willingness to let your breath deeply nourish you on the inhale, and to completely let go on the exhale. With this attitude you are living deeply during each phase of the breath cycle.

A mental conditioning program for athletes

by Barry K. Weinhold, Ph.D.

In almost every sport athletes complain about having "on" and "off" days, about reaching plateaus that are not what they themselves define as their fully functioning level. Until recently the emphasis has been to search for the causes of this problem in the physical conditioning program of the athlete and, to some extent, in his or her diet and nutrition. Much has been written about the type of physical conditioning program best for each athlete, and some books have begun to cover diet and nutrition. Until recently not much attention has been given to the role of the mental conditioning of the athlete and the effects of a good or poor mental condition. Gallwey (1976) developed one of the first systems for incorporating mental principles in the teaching of tennis. Since then some of these principles have been applied to skiing (Fowler & Smith, 1977) and jogging/running (Sheehan, 1978).

The basic assumption of this chapter is that the fully functioning athlete must have a program for good physical conditioning, for good nutrition, and for good mental conditioning. The diagram below illustrates this relationship.

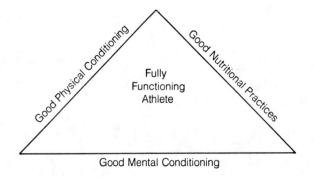

There are many sources of information about good physical conditioning and good nutritional practices. This chapter, therefore, focuses on the often neglected principles of mental conditioning as applied to the sports of tennis, skiing, and running. All three sports can be engaged in on a purely recreational basis, or they can be competitive, professional activities.

THE PROHIBITION AGAINST KNOWING YOURSELF

Socrates admonished his followers with the phrase "know thyself," probably because many people he knew didn't know themselves very well. Things don't seem much different today. There seems to be a persistent belief that what you don't know about yourself can't hurt you, which by definition means that people are afraid to know themselves. Unless you are willing to explore your own inner space, what you are unaware of can hurt you. Knowing yourself includes understanding the relationship between the quality of your thoughts and the quality of results in all areas of your life, as well as understanding the role your feelings play in achieving these results.

Most athletes who don't break the prohibition against knowing themselves may have to contend with an internal environment that consists of the following:

1. FEAR

    "I'm afraid we are going to lose."

    "I'm afraid I'm never going to get any better."

    "I'm afraid I'm not playing well."

    "I'm afraid I'll make stupid mistakes."

    "If I goof up they [teammates, coaches, fans] won't like me."

    "What if I choke at a crucial time?"

2. LACK OF SELF-CONFIDENCE

    "I don't believe I can improve."

"*I never win the big ones.*"

"*My opponent is better than I.*"

"*I'm too old, too slow, too short, too tall, [and so on].*"

3. SELF-CONDEMNATION
"*I always screw up things.*"

"*That was a dumb shot.*"

"*I should have known better.*"

4. POOR CONCENTRATION
"*I can't keep my mind on what I'm doing.*"

"*It's hard to get really absorbed.*"

"*I get in a groove and then 'bang' I lose it.*"

5. TRYING TOO HARD
"*The harder I try, the worse I get.*"

"*I can't seem to relax out there.*"

6. LACK OF WILLINGNESS TO WIN IN COMPETITIVE SPORTS
"*I can't get pumped up for the game or match.*"

"*I lack the killer instinct.*"

"*I feel better when I am losing.*"

7. PERFECTIONISM
"*I am never content with my performance.*"

"*I'll never be as good as I want to be.*"

8. SELF-CONSCIOUSNESS
"*I am always self-conscious about how I'm doing.*"

9. FRUSTRATION
"*I can't shake off a mistake.*"

"*I feel like quitting when I miss a shot.*"

10. ANGER AND BLAME
"*I am so mad at myself I can't think.*"

"*The referee is calling them wrong. He can't see straight.*"

"*How can he [opponent] do that to me?*"

"*The coach is always picking on me.*"

11. BOREDOM

"It's hard to get excited about this anymore."

"It isn't much fun any more."

12. EXPECTATIONS

"I never can reach the coach's expectations of me."

"I guess I just don't expect enough of myself."

13. A BUSY MIND

"I am too busy thinking about what to do to actually do it."

"I try to remember everything I've learned but I can't."

It is no wonder that your performance suffers if you can identify with a number of the preceding mental barriers. It may seem discouraging to try to overcome these mental barriers, but the mental reconditioning process is simple and straightforward. Like physical conditioning, mental conditioning takes time and practice.

THE CHARACTERISTICS OF A MENTALLY CONDITIONED ATHLETE

Good mental conditioning involves regular use of a number of processes and activities. Through repeated practice of these activities, good mental conditioning begins to emerge. These activities and processes are grouped into the five important areas of focus necessary for good mental conditioning. They are: (1) a focus on purpose and priorities, (2) a focus on contribution, (3) a focus on strengths instead of weaknesses, (4) a focus on core problems and issues, and (5) a focus on planning (Drucker, 1974). Each of these areas is explained and a number of activities and processes presented in this chapter.

A Focus on Purpose and Priorities

Why are you playing tennis? What does running do for you? How does skiing fit into your overall purpose in life? It is often surprising that many people actually don't know why they are doing what they are doing. The activity may have become a ritualized part of life and the original purpose for starting it forgotten or changed without conscious awareness. Peer pressure, "keeping up with the Joneses," "everyone's doing it," or keeping in shape are often surface reasons that the recreational skiier or jogger or tennis player gets caught in. Help may be needed to refocus the purpose. The mentally conditioned athlete knows exactly why he/she is playing a sport and how it fits into his/her overall purpose in life. Such athletes have the big picture, and therefore their wants and goals are derived directly from this context. They are often seen by others who lack this overall focus as single-minded, directed, focused, certain, clear, and purposeful in their playing. One person who clearly has developed that context said, "One of the reasons I play tennis is because it helps me learn to stay in the 'here and now,' which is my overall purpose in life. If I am over-hitting my ground strokes and getting out ahead of the ball, it usually means I'm ahead of myself in other aspects of my life as well, or at least that my mind is somewhere in the future and not focused on what I am doing now. When I notice this, I practice letting go of any and all thoughts that take me away from the present. As I do that, I notice that my tendency to overhit shots disappears, and I am hitting the ball where I want to. This is also true if I am late in my swing. I usually can trace that to some leftover thoughts from earlier in the day which I haven't let go of."

The following activities and processes will help you develop in context for whatever sport or activity you participate in.

Clarifying Your Purpose in Life

RATIONALE   Your first task as a mentally conditioned athlete is to have a clear purpose for your life that is broad enough to include everything you do. Your purpose is defined as the overall context against which all experiences can be measured. In this way, you can always check how purposeful you are in whatever you are doing.

STEP 1   Take a blank paper and write the following open-ended sentence on it: "My purpose in life is _____. Complete that sentence with as few words as you can that pull together all aspects of your life. An example of a statement of purpose is "My purpose in life is to experience each moment and activity as completely as possible from a 'here and now' focus."

STEP 2   Take your completed statement of purpose and ask yourself the following questions:

> "Is this statement broad enough to include everything I do?"
>
> "Will I ever complete my purpose?" (Purpose goes on infinitely.)
>
> "Is it clear enough so I could explain it to someone else and that person would understand?"
>
> "Is it written in simple terms?"
>
> "Is the statement reduced to its basic level?"

If your answer is "no" to any of those questions, then continue rewriting your statement of purpose until you feel satisfied with it.

Note: You may need to repeat these two activities from time to time to see if you are stabilized or changing in your purpose.

What Are Your Intentions?

RATIONALE   Your intentions or wants are the motivating forces or desires that take you from your purpose to setting specific goals. Examples are "I want to run an eight-minute mile" or "I want to learn to parallel ski down most slopes."

STEP 1   Step 1 involves generating as many specific wants relative to the specific sport as you can. Make up a list of wants by repeatedly writing the open-ended sentence: "I want to _____." (For example, "I want to play tennis twice a week," etc.)

STEP 2   Now go back over each want you have listed in Step 1 and place a check mark (√) beside those wants that seem to support your purpose and a question mark (?) next to those that you aren't sure about.

STEP 3   Now examine those wants you aren't sure about and how they support your purpose. Try to change them so they do support your purpose. If you can't get them to support your purpose, cross them out.

Achieving Results through Goal Setting

RATIONALE   Goals are ways of measuring how purposeful you are in an area of your life at a given time. By setting a goal, you are making it possible to achieve your intentions and realize your purpose in life. For example, if your intention is to be an "A" tennis player within a year, you must set specific daily, weekly, and monthly goals to enable you to realize your intention.

STEP 1   Keeping in mind the sport you used in the previous activity, write a letter to a friend dated one year from today's date. Tell this friend all the things you have accomplished relative to that sport during the past year. Be specific and fantasize about all the things you think might be possible to accomplish during the next year. State them in the letter *as if* they have already been completed.

STEP 2   Now take the letter and extract specific goal statements for the year. For example, "I have become an 'A' tennis player."

STEP 3   Now take these specific goal statements for the year and back them up to six months from now. Write specific statements about where you expect to be in six months (e.g., "I now am a high 'B' tennis player.") Then reduce each of these goal statements to three-month and one-month goal statements. You can reduce them further to weekly or daily goals if you wish. Planning and time management strategies for developing weekly and daily goals are discussed later.

STEP 4   After you have broken down each goal, examine it again and decide whether or not you are willing to put forth the energy to reach that goal. You may wish to eliminate or change some goals based on this breakdown.

Concentration Training

One of the most powerful tools of the mentally conditioned athlete is his or her ability to concentrate (Weinhold & Elliott, 1979). Mental concentration exercises can aid the athlete who has trouble staying focused on a specific task or skill. The ability to be deeply aware of what you are doing and not to be distracted by internal and external interferences is difficult to learn.

RATIONALE   It would be simple if we could just decide to concentrate. We need to train our minds to concentrate, and a powerful training tool is the activity of sitting, which is used by many athletes to help them learn to stay focused on their task.

STEP 1   Sit in a comfortable position with your eyes closed, your back straight, and your feet flat on the floor. Breathe normally and rest your hands in your lap.

STEP 2   Give your complete attention to the rising and falling of your abdomen as you breathe. You do not have to say the words "rising and falling." Simply focus your attention on your abdomen as it rises and falls during normal breathing. As you do this, your mind will inevitably drift off on other thoughts, feelings, or sensations. As you notice this happening, just be aware of these distractions and *without judgment* return your focus to the rising and falling of your abdomen.

STEP 3   Develop an awareness of when you are being pulled off your focus and then quickly return to your primary focus. The quicker you notice distractions, the quicker you can let go of them.

STEP 4   Your mind will wander, so don't be dismayed by how difficult this task is at first. It is important not to judge yourself for having these distractions; practice not making any critical judgments.

STEP 5   Start with at least 10 to 15 minutes of practice once a day, and then increase the time as your concentration improves. Some athletes find that they require as much as an hour a day of this or similar activities for concentration training. The results you can expect in addition to improved concentration are a relaxed calmness, an improved awareness of everything going on inside and outside of you *without* being distracted by anything that is happening, and finally new insights and creative thoughts that will surface as you let go of the usual mental "clutter."

The Art of Forgetting Who You Are

Any sport can be a way of practicing forgetting who you are. If you are too self-conscious, it is likely that you will not perform well. Most meditative and concentration practices such as the one just described have as an objective the freeing of the individual from self-monitoring. The trick is to let go of those thoughts you have about yourself and what you are doing and *just do it*. Skiing from that point of view means letting the body and muscles respond to the moment. If you can do this without the interference of conscious thoughts about yourself, skiing can be intoxicatingly fun.

A Focus on Contribution

The second focus necessary for good mental conditioning is a focus on contribution. To achieve this focus it is necessary to develop a "you and me" orientation to sports instead of a "you or me" orientation. In an interview (Poppy, 1979) about his Breakthrough Racing Project Werner Erhard says: "Part of our inadequacy comes from our having been committed for so long to the notion of 'you or me' that we don't have patterns of thought, or behavior, or even the possibility of 'you *and* me' [p. 4]."

Dyveke Spino teaches tennis using a "you *and* me" orientation. She pays vigorous attention to weight training and aerobic conditioning, but she contends that most tennis players injure themselves not because they aren't in shape but because they are overly aggressive. Many people play tennis from a hostile "you or me" attitude, not knowing there is another way (Leonard, 1977).

To develop a "you and me" attitude, do the following activities with your partner before playing tennis.

Calming the Waters

RATIONALE   The purpose of this activity is to create a context for playing tennis together that allows a "you *and* me" orientation to emerge.

STEP 1   Sit quietly together for five minutes or so before you step on the court. Without touching each other, each of you close your eyes and imagine a waterfall of light flowing gently down from the top of your head through your entire body, filling your body with calming, relaxing light energy. Keep breathing and let your breath send the light energy to each and every part of your body to calm and relax you completely.

STEP 2   When both of you have relaxed yourselves completely with light energy, then expand this energy to join with your partner's energy. Feel the flow of calm, relaxed light energy between you, bringing both of you into harmony.

STEP 3   Now expand your energy to include the court you will be playing on. Visualize this court as being a calm, clear pool of energy. Feel your combined energy washing over the court, cleansing the energy on it. Remember that no matter how wild and erratic the energy is on the other courts around yours, your court will remain a still pool of energy during the time you are playing on it.

STEP 4   Now picture your court and picture yourself and your partner stepping onto the court. Picture yourself warming up by hitting perfect shots back and forth to your partner. First, talk to your partner about each kind of shot you are going to practice. Take about 30 seconds to practice each kind of shot mentally. Start with ground strokes, first forehand and then backhand, each time picturing yourself and your partner making smooth perfect shots to each other. Do the same for overheads, drop shots, and serves. Feel yourself move as you hit the ball. See the ball hit the racquet on each shot. Hear the sound of the ball hitting that "sweet spot" of the racquet and going exactly where you want it to go. (Note! If during a match you find yourself losing this image, stop and go through Step 4 again with your partner.)

STEP 5 Now with your eyes open and relaxed move onto the court and begin to practice the shots again that you imagined in Step 4, first without a racquet and then with a racquet but without hitting the ball. Do this for several minutes.

STEP 6 Now you are ready to start actually hitting the ball. What you will likely find is that your shots are exactly as you imagined them and very little actual warm-up is necessary for you to be ready to play. If you start hitting poor shots return to the image you created and watch your shots improve.

STEP 7 As you begin playing think of your well-hit ball as a gift of energy given to your partner to be returned and exchanged between you, linking you with your partner in a single energy field. To aid this process, synchronize your breathing. When you hit the ball, exhale and inhale as the ball is returned.

STEP 8 By agreement with your partner, you may want to strengthen the energy field between you by hitting the ball to each other's weakest area. In this way, you can help each other improve and strengthen the energy field between you.

A Focus on Strengths

Strengths are the focus of the athlete who is practicing mental conditioning. As said earlier in the chapter, many athletes focus on negative thinking as a means of improvement rather than on positive thoughts. Thoughts are a form of energy. Similar to the use of imagery in the previous activity, positive thoughts will lead to positive results, and negative thoughts will lead to negative results.

One of the most powerful tools of good mental conditioning is permission. A permission is a positive thought or message that supports any positive changes. Permissions say to you, "Yes, you can do it," instead of "why try?" You can give yourself permissions, you can get them from others, and they are available in the environment (Weinhold & Andresen, 1979).

The following story written by Mary Drew illustrates how permissions can come from unexpected sources when you most need them.

THE MARATHON

I remember glancing up at the sky and feeling thankful that it was overcast. Clouds meant shade, and shade hopefully meant coolness. It was the morning of my first marathon and I was feeling apprehensive. Friends surrounded me with encouraging words, final thoughts and anticipating silence. I knew this was it. The day I had been training for, working for, hoping for. It had finally arrived.

Before I could let the anticipation soak in, a sea of humanity began rolling down the road. The race had begun! Think slow I reminded myself, think slow. I had a tendency in training to pace myself too rapidly and needed extra reminding to slow down. As I fell into my pace, I mentally renewed all the reasons for my running in this marathon. Positive thoughts are the key to my success.

The crowds were great, their nourishment and encouragement continually spurred me into new limits of energy. I felt great at mile 10. This was the first time I had begun to notice the sun, it felt warm but I felt good. It wasn't until mile 15 that I began to notice the old ankle injury. Before the race started, I had that nagging sensation of having forgotten something. I should have wrapped the ankle for this race, but it was too late now to dwell on my mistake. I never before realized the amazing power the mind has over physical achievement. I now understood what world class runners mean when they claim you must be mentally prepared for a race as well as physically.

At mile 22 I was confronted with very strange negative feelings. My ankle was still aching and my side had developed a stitch. *My mind began telling me I had to stop, there was no way I was going to complete this race. Every muscle in my body seemed to tighten up. I recall stopping at a water station and hearing the crowd cheering me to continue on. Frustrated, I looked mercifully to them and admitted my uncertainties about completing the race. My next thoughts recall being taken quickly by the arm by an unfamiliar woman. She determinedly stared me straight in the eyes, and as she led me she said, "Mary, you are a winner and I'm going to help you finish this race!"*

If anyone were to ask me where I was the last four miles of the race, I honestly couldn't tell them. This extraordinary woman and I went on a trip, a voyage into unexplored fibers of strength and desire. Her voice soothed me and calmed me. This wonderful stranger was my companion, my friend.

Slowly turning up the final street towards the finish line, I began to re-enter reality and began to recognize familiar faces. Tears entered my eyes as I came closer to the end of my journey. My friend began to break away from me. "Let's cross the finish line together," I exclaimed, feeling very emotional over the experience we had shared together. "I can't," she stated, "I don't have a number, I'm a spectator." She slowly broke her pace with me and as she blended into the crowd she yelled, "You're a winner Mary, we are all winners!"

I was never able to discover the identity of this woman, nor was I ever able to see her again. I will always remember her as a strong positive force for me, not only in running, but in my life. I was a winner, she was a winner, we are all winners. Whenever I close my eyes, I will always be able to grasp the moment of it all and smile.

Permission Checklist

RATIONALE This checklist is designed to increase your awareness of important permissions that you might be wanting but are unaware of wanting. If you identify with any of the permissions in the checklist, you can give these to yourself ("Take your time and pace yourself"), ask for others to give them to you ("Will you tell me that it's OK for me to take my time?"), or notice them in your environment (seeing others taking their time or watching how slowly and deliberately your cat is moving when she walks).

STEP 1 Fill out the following checklist. Place a check mark beside those items you believe would be helpful to you to remember and use while playing sports.

_____ *I am important. I belong here.*

_____ *I can take my time to learn this sport.*

_____ *I can relax while playing this sport.*

_____ *I can make mistakes and learn from them.*

_____ *I can play and have fun.*

_____ *I am fine just the way I am.*

_____ *I can be successful.*

_____ *I can ask for what I want from others.*

_____ *I can come in first.*

_____ *I can be spontaneous and creative.*

_____ *I can take care of myself.*

_____ *I can enjoy what I am doing.*

_____ *I can change what I am doing if I want to.*

_____ *I can _____ [Fill in your own permissions].*

STEP 2 Examine the permissions you checked and decide how you are going to get those permissions. The best way to think about these permissions is in the present tense. "I can relax while playing this sport" needs to be changed to "I am relaxed while playing this sport."

STEP 3 Take a sheet of paper and draw a line down the page about two-thirds of the way across, making two columns. On the left side of the line write the permission as instructed in Step 2, and on the right side write any negating thoughts you are aware of. For example: "I am relaxed while playing tennis."

| *"I am relaxed while playing tennis."* | *"You get uptight when you miss an easy shot."* |

Continue writing the permission and bringing to the surface any negative thoughts until you can write the permission without any additional negative thoughts coming to your awareness.

Permissions are an important tool to help you focus on strengths. Every new record is set by athletes who have conditioned their minds to see the possibility of achieving that record. Until Roger Bannister broke the "four-minute barrier" most runners thought it was impossible to run a four-minute mile. Now it is accomplished regularly by world class runners. What he accomplished gave others the permission to break any four-minute barrier they had subconsciously created.

A Focus on Generic Problem Solving

The mentally conditioned athlete has just as many problems to solve as an athlete who hasn't conditioned his or her mind. The difference is that a mentally conditioned athlete has developed effective processes for uncovering any underlying or generic problem present in the problem situation, and then solves that problem. The poorly conditioned athlete may be led astray by the problem elements of the situation and therefore not see the forest for the trees.

All problems except the unique ones require a generic solution. The development of a rule or a principle is required to solve a generic problem. One common problem that many runners face is the so-called "wall" that develops when the runner has to deal with physical pain that grows out of reaching perceived physical limits. Most runners believe that the way to solve that problem is to train harder and gradually push themselves through the "wall." Some runners never solve this problem and give up; others take a long time to break this barrier. In analyzing this problem and looking for a generic principle to use to solve it, ask yourself the following several questions:

- What is basic to the problem?
- What are probably only symptoms of the problem?
- How long am I willing to let this be a problem?
- What would be different if the problem were solved?
- What, if anything, am I willing to compromise on or give up in order to solve this problem?
- How will I know if I have solved this problem?
- What resources do I have that can help me solve this problem?
- Do I know other people who have solved this problem successfully?
- What are the common elements of the solutions others have used?

Using some of these questions, you might conclude that what is basic to your problem is, "I can't breathe fully enough to get through that barrier." You might begin to understand what causes shortness of breath. Is it a lack of training? "No!" Is it fear of the situation? "Yes!" Now you have the beginning of a principle: "When I get afraid, my breathing gets more shallow." So the possible generic solution is to deal with the fear of the physical symptoms you are aware of when you "hit the wall." What do the symptoms mean? Can you get accurate information to help you overcome these fears? Maybe you believe you will die if you go on or that you will do serious damage to your body. Is that true? Then you can test your principle: "If I relax and continue breathing fully and completely when I hit the wall, I will go through it without any harmful effects." You can mentally picture yourself hitting the wall, feeling the symptoms, and then relaxing as a way of practicing the process before physically doing it.

Scar Awareness

RATIONALE   The purpose of this activity is to analyze the generic problems that may have been present at a time when you injured yourself. By recalling the situation, you may uncover the generic problem which, if solved, will prevent repetitive injuries.

STEP 1   Make a list of scars on your body caused by a sports-related injury. List them by the side (left or right) of the body on which they are located. Make another list of previous injuries that left no scar. Again, organize the list by left and right side.

STEP 2   Now apply the following set of principles in examining the lists. Principle 1: Scars and injuries to the left side of the body are caused by not paying attention to feelings, and conversely scars and injuries on the right side of the body are caused by not thinking clearly. Principle 2: Scars and injuries to the left side are related to violating rules set down by your mother (or the most significant female in your life), and injuries to the right side are caused by violating rules set down initially by your father (or the most significant male in your life). For example, your mother may have said, "Don't show off," and you may have fallen and scraped your left knee as the result of showing off. The principle is that the left side relates to the feminine side and the right side to masculine issues or direction.

A Focus on Planning

The ultimate use of your mind is to develop for yourself the best possible program of nutrition, exercise, and positive mental attitude. This obviously requires thoughtful planning. The best plan grows naturally out of your overall purpose in life and remains within this context.

A model for this planning follows. It shows a daily, weekly, and monthly planning and clearing program for tennis and can be used for singles or doubles. This model can be adapted for use with any athletic activity and incorporates the areas of focus developed in this chapter.

Planning and Clearing Process

RATIONALE By using a systematic method for planning and for clearing any barriers, you have a greater chance of accomplishing your goals and realizing your purpose. This process can be modified to fit your given situation.

STEP 1 Get together with your partner [person(s)] you are playing with in doubles or singles. Develop a framework for playing tennis that includes completing a number of the activities from this chapter and then discussing them.

STEP 2 Set up a time schedule for practice, planning, and playing with your partner(s). It is important to build in time to complete the Planning and Clearing Sheet and discuss the result with your partner(s).

STEP 3 Complete the Planning and Clearing Sheet that follows.

TENNIS WEEKLY PLANNING AND CLEARING SHEET

Name _____ Week No. _____ From _____ To _____

Monthly Goal _____

Overall Goal for this Week _____

1. How I feel about tennis right now is:

_____

(Remember: list feelings, not thoughts.)

2. Are there any:

	With Self	With Partner	With Opposing Players
incomplete items	_____	_____	_____
unresolved conflicts	_____	_____	_____
broken agreements	_____	_____	_____
undelivered communications	_____	_____	_____
lies or withheld criticisms	_____	_____	_____

If so, list only one in each category and decide what you are willing to do about each one. _____

3. Is there anything in between me and feeling absolutely great about my tennis?

_____

If so, what is it? (be specific):

_____

4. One way to expand my enjoyment of tennis this week is (be specific):

_____

5. Three things I can picture myself completing successfully this week are (be specific):

_____

_____

_____

6. Assign dates and priorities by which I intend to complete them:

_____

7. One thing I will do to take total responsibility for the success of my tennis program is:

_____

8. My self-permission for the week is:

_____

9. One way I will increase the quality of my tennis is:

_____

10. Daily mental conditioning (do the following every day):

I acknowledge myself for _____

I forgive myself for _____

I forgive _____ for _____

I am grateful for _____

My new and creative idea for the day is _____

_____

Weekly Report and Reflection Time: This is done weekly with partner(s) verbally or in writing (exchange reports).

1. What worked best for me this week was:

_____

142

2. What I thought didn't work for me this week was:

_____

3. What got in my way the most this week was:

_____

4. My personal effectiveness quotient was (refer to overall goal and three specific goals):

	Goal	Result	Rate Your Effectiveness (Result—Goal)
Overall	_____	_____	_____
1	_____	_____	_____
2	_____	_____	_____
3	_____	_____	_____

5. One thing I will do to increase my results next week is:

_____

6. One thing or area I will picture doing successfully next week is:

_____

7. How I will do that is _____

8. What you (_____) can do to support me is:
              name

_____

_____

9. The suggestions, comments, or acknowledgments I have for you are:

_____

_____

10. Time spent on tennis-related activities this week:

_____

11. My priorities for next week are:

_____

_____

I am grateful for the progress I made this week and give thanks for all that I have.

_____

POSTSCRIPT

There are many techniques for gaining control over those mental processes necessary for good mental conditioning. A few of them have been presented in this chapter. The ultimate goal of any well-conditioned athlete is to transcend his or her conditioning. This means letting go and "being" instead of concentrating on "doing" something. In most martial arts the master and the beginner are seen as close together. That is, the master has transcended technique, and the beginner knows no technique. Therefore, both are free from the restrictions of technique. The same is true in all athletic endeavors. The highly skilled professional is able to get his mind out of the way so thinking isn't necessary—only reacting in well-trained ways. Thinking takes too much time. The training has to provide reactions to all situations or at least a built-in process for developing instantly successful solutions to unforeseen problems or challenges.

All athletes are aware that not everything can be foreseen or planned for. Yet the successful athlete seems to be able to respond to the unforeseen with a set of movements that could not be thought out in advance. It is my contention that those athletes who have cleared out their mental blocks or barriers and who are basically "on purpose" or purposeful in their lives are better able to respond successfully to the unforeseen in life and in sports.

BIBLIOGRAPHY

CRATTY, BRYANT J. AND HANIN, YURI L. *The Athlete in the Sports Team*. Denver: Love Publishing Co., 1980.

DRUCKER, PETER F. *The Effective Executive* New York: Harper & Row, 1967.

FOWLER, CORKY AND SMITH, CHRISTOPHER. *The Hidden Skier*. Chicago: Contemporary Books, 1977.

GALLWAY, W. TIMOTHY. *Inner Tennis*. New York: Random House, 1976.

LEONARD, GEORGE. *The Ultimate Athlete*. New York: Avon Books, 1977.

POPPY, JOHN. "Breakthrough Racing: An Interview with Werner Erhard." Reprinted from *The Graduate Review* (July 1979), pp. 1–8.

SHAPIRO, DEANE H., JR. *Precision Nirvana*. Englewood Cliffs, N.J.: Prentice-Hall, 1978.

SHEEHAN, GEORGE. *Running and Being*. New York: Warner Books, 1978.

SIMONTON, CARLO, SIMONTON-MATTHEWS, STEPHANIE AND CREIGHTON, JAMES L. *Getting Well Again*. New York: Bantam Books, 1980.

WEINHOLD, BARRY AND ANDRESEN, GAIL. *Threads: Unraveling the Mysteries of Adult Life*. New York: Richard Marek, 1979.

WEINHOLD, BARRY AND ELLIOTT, LYNN. *Transpersonal Communication*. Englewood Cliffs, N.J.: Prentice-Hall, 1979.

The
centered walker

We come now to our final chapter. It is fitting that we should end by considering walking, which is how most of us began to use our bodies in the first place. In many ways walking is the ultimate sport. It needs no paraphernalia, it is simple and easy, and it brings a world of satisfaction to even the most desultory practitioner.

Walking is the ideal sport for centering—it sets the body a-tingle and clears the mind. Colin Fletcher, who walked through the Grand Canyon, described a walk he often takes a few minutes from his city apartment:

> Up there, alone with the wind and sky and the steep grassy slopes, I nearly always find after a while that I am beginning to think more clearly. Yet "think" does not seem to be quite the right word. Sometimes when it is a matter of making a choice, I do not believe I decide what to do so much as discover what I have decided. It is as if my mind, set free by space and solitude and oiled by the body's easy rhythm, swings open and releases thoughts it has formulated. Sometimes, when I have been straining too hard to impose order on an urgent press of ideas, it seems only as if my mind has slowly relaxed; then, all at once, there is room for the ideas to fall into place in a meaningful pattern.*

The movements of the body, the swing of arms and stride of legs, are a perfect rhythm that quiets the mind and allows one to come to the creative space within.

*From The New Complete Walker, Second Edition, Revised, Enlarged, and Updated by Colin Fletcher. Copyright © 1968, 1974 by Colin Fletcher. Reprinted by permission of Alfred A. Knopf, Inc.

Those who have literary aspirations would do well to note that walking was a favorite activity of Wordsworth, De Quincey, Coleridge, Cowper, and Carlyle, among others. Ben Jonson walked all the way from London to Scotland, and while there is no direct evidence that his friend Shakespeare was a walker, Shakespeare observed a relationship between walking and a "merry heart." His line, "Jog on, jog on, the footpath way," could also be an aphorism for our times.

Most athletes put away their gear come sundown, content to think about sports or watch them on television. Recently, though, with indoor tracks and racquet courts the athlete has been able to get a workout in the evening. Walkers, though, have been going out in the night for many years, and finding it peaceful, healthful, and full of opportunities for contemplation.

Several famous writers have remarked on the benefits of night walking. In Charles Dickens's famous essay, "Night Walks," he mentions that he began walking at night because he could not sleep. What he experienced on the streets could hardly have been better than tossing and turning.

In a short breathing space I was on Westminster-bridge, regaling my houseless eyes with the external walls of the British Parliament—the perfection of a stupendous institution, I know, and the admiration of all surrounding nations and succeeding ages, I do not doubt, but perhaps a little the better now and then for being pricked up to its work. Turning off into Old Palace-yard, the Courts of Law kept me company for a quarter of an hour; hinting in low whispers what numbers of people they were keeping awake, and how intensely wretched and horrible they were rendering the small hours to unfortunate suitors. Westminster Abbey was fine gloomy society for another quarter of an hour; suggesting a wonderful procession of its dead among the dark arches and pillars, each century more amazed by the century following it than by all the centuries going before. And indeed in those houseless night walks—which even included cemeteries where watchmen went round among the graves at stated times, and moved the tell-tale handle of an index which recorded that they had touched it at such an hour—it was a solemn consideration what enormous hosts of dead belong to one old great city, and how, if they were raised while the living slept, there would not be the space of a pin's point in all the streets and ways for the living to come out into. Not only that, but armies of dead would overflow the hills and valleys beyond the city, and would stretch away all round it, God knows how far.

For some, the night walk provides an occasion for self-revelation. The night, and the darker part of us all, must eventually be confronted. We must come to terms with the negative—fear, anger, avarice, and their cousins—to embrace the whole. By being willing to deal with the beasts within we get the opportunity to embrace the positive. To deny the one is to deny the other; when we greet all of ourselves, even the parts we loathe, we establish a relationship with ourselves that is accepting and generous. Ultimately it is not how we feel that is important (for who will ever be without the negative emotions?); it is how we feel about how we feel. In other words, positive and negative feelings will come and go like the tides, and if we maintain an open and accepting attitude toward all our feelings we have the opportunity for a most loving relationship with ourselves and thereby with the world around us.

If night does not deter the serious walker, neither should weather, for each season has its charms for the foot traveler. The experience of winter—the crunch of snow underfoot, the silence, the rosy cheeks—can be as beautiful to the walker as spring, with its blossoms and promise of bounty, or the crisp air of autumn that energizes and urges one on. No one needs to be told about summer, when most walkers take to the trails, but we often mistakenly put away our walking shoes during the other seasons.

Be sensible but adventurous. Walk in all seasons and experience all types of weather. Learn to participate and appreciate the many sides of life.

As Emerson said, "Walking has the best value as gymnastics for the mind." During a walk the mind clears, the feelings surface and subside, the mind learns to function in harmony with the body.

Many of us spend so much of our time thinking, reasoning, worrying, hoping, that we do not experience life as it is. A walk

can be an experiment in letting go of the chatter between the ears
and hearing what is really going on inside.

As one gifted poet said:

On a walk one day I
began acknowledging the
truth about myself.
  I'm angry
  I like to be treated nicely
  I feel scared
  I have a red car
  I like to be loved
  I need to be needed
  I have some things I
    need to talk to _____
    about
Then the healing began. As
soon as I had acknowledged
the truth, a flow of
spontaneous realizations
began about how to handle
each situation.
  I can tell _____ the
  truth about the situation
  as I see it.
  I can love myself for
  feeling scared.
  It's all right to want love.
Then a quiet bliss began
inside, waves of feeling
in my body coupled
with feelings of space and
expansion in my mind.
I rose up out of my inhibited,
tucked-in posture, and
breathed anew, the
dry, crisp air of a
mountain autumn.
  And all this in the space
  of a quarter mile!

And consider the following enlightening experience of a female foot traveler, Carol Leavenworth.

Walking played an important part in one of the most intense periods of growth I have ever experienced. A short walk, less than two miles, marked the beginning of two weeks of insight into the nature of life and my own place in the greater scheme of things.

I am not an avid walker or sportsperson of any sort. Generally walking is too slow and boring. I do not enjoy the mundane turn my thoughts take on a walk alone or the kind of rhythmic repetition I experience as foot, breath and thought reflect one another's movement during walking. One early summer Monday I was three days into an extended absence of husband and children. I had looked forward to being alone in the house with both excitement and some apprehension. I would be free of all demands and schedules—but how well, how happily would I use this time.

At first I accepted invitations and went out among friends. Somehow this felt uncomfortable, yet when I remained alone I was lonely and uneasy. On the day of the walk I had a luncheon appointment with a close friend. I decided to set out early, being at loose ends in the house and to walk to the downtown restaurant to fill the time until our meeting.

As I started out I had the same unpleasant and colorless thoughts that generally plagued my mind on a walk alone. I cast around for an interesting train of thought and suddenly remembered a Buddhist walking Meditation I had read about several years previously. I decided to try it as I remembered it to be very simple. It involved naming each activity one becomes aware of and simply repeating the name without any further mental comment. So I began "Walking . . . walking. . ." I repeated to myself. "This is even more boring," I thought and then caught myself and repeated, "Thinking . . . thinking. . ." I noticed a bird's song, "Hearing . . . listening. . ." I said to myself. I saw flowers and trees and sky and repeated, "Seeing . . . looking . . . watching. . ." As my awareness of my body and mind shifted moment-by-moment so did the activity I named; "breathing" replaced "stepping . . . walking. . ." or "thinking" from time to time as the basic activity although obviously all were occurring together. It became clear in only a few blocks that it is impossible to be aware of even the simplest activity in its wholeness and its depth at one moment. We shine the spotlight of our attention to illuminate our lives and by doing so cast the greater part into even deeper shadow.

This was the nature of the thoughts that began to rush through my mind in competition with my naming meditation. Not so boring yet I still found the exercise to be the most excruciatingly dull walk I have ever experienced. At the halfway point I considered dropping the meditation, but I continued it by choosing to see my thoughts as an expected expression of the resistance that can be found in any growth experience.

By the time I reached the restaurant I was electrified by the richness and variety of my inner experience. Every sight, sound, and smell had an intensity and beauty that was nearly psychedelic. My thoughts—creeping in between the naming activity of the meditation—were increasingly profound and varied. Each breath I took felt like I was inhaling nectar. I passed up the wine at lunch. I was already drunk on experience.

This walk was followed by two weeks of deep contentment and highly energized mental activity. I saw many questions that had been puzzling me in a new light. One after another, issues that had been confusing and frustrating fell into order in my mind. As the days passed and the time for my family to return approached I faced the anxiety of what seemed to be a major transition for me. I did not want things to change; I wanted to stay forever in this state of peaceful suspension of time watching the secrets of the world unfold effortlessly before me. Yet the tide of change is relentless–there was no holding back and I knew it. I made a plan, took a deep breath and greeted the returning hoard with a smile.

As I look back I see that the following month was perhaps the most intense and concentrated period of action and creativity I have ever experienced. There was little time for peaceful contemplation—all was furious activity.

I had coped, created, provided balance, and transcended an unusually large number of events and activities apparently effortlessly. Even I felt only pleasantly stretched and challenged under circumstances that at any other time would have severely taxed my patience and energy.

Since that time I have used the walking meditation to clear out the cobwebs in times of stress and frustration. It has never failed to help me relax and focus and somehow transcend whatever confusion I had experienced. Doors open in my mind, the difficult becomes possible and the impossible becomes merely challenging. And it all begins with a walk.

For the walker who seeks variety on the footpath variations can be made on the basic brisk walk. There is the amble, the saunter, the lope, and the rove. While definitions of the first three paces can be found in a good dictionary, the rove is too recent an invention to have an official definition. It was invented by Jon H. Leonard, Jack L. Hofer, and Nathan Pritikin in their book called *Live Longer Now*, and is a combination of walking and running. The rules are simple: Walk until you feel like running, then run until you feel like walking. With the rove, a variation of the Boy Scout pace in which you run 50 steps and then walk 50 steps, it is possible to cover a great deal of ground at a clip that is perfectly suited to you.

Walking and centering go hand in hand. The poet Garrett Martin summed it up well:

As I walked out one morning
I found that I was one,
And as I walked further
I found all others were too.

To come into an awareness of our own oneness, and to find our oneness with all else in life, we need only set forth on the path with the correct intention. If we set our minds so that each moment, whether on the field of play or on the larger field of life, will bring us closer to our true selves and our true path, then we turn each moment into an adventure of learning, brotherhood, and unity: the very experience of centering.

Index